PAST THE GOAL LINE

Dave Walton, Author

CREATESPACE.COM

ISBN-13:978-1977531094
ISBN-10:1977531091

Dave Walton, Author

Publisher: www.HoltPublishing.Yolasite.com
Editor: Janice Sharek

DAVE "JUNIOR" WALTON

I once focused on running the football past the goal line to score. With Heaven as our focus, I challenge you to carry many souls past the finish line.

Romans 1:16
I am not ashamed of the gospel.

Dave "Junior" Walton

DEDICATION

Honoring Men where Honor is Due

ALEXANDER WALTON... My Daddy always encouraged me in sports to "give it all you got." He believed an athlete should be in great physical condition and this can only be achieved by difficult training and by pushing yourself beyond your physical limits. Never quit! Dad would become my greatest cheerleader and inspire me to always give it my best. Daddy and I came to faith in Jesus Christ "together" on September 7, 1975. What a great gift God gave to us!

COACH JIMMY YORK... Coach York was my elementary school coach and teacher. Coach York is a legend in his own right, and taught me to believe I could play any sport. He said to always practice hard and to make good school grades.

COACH GILBERT COX... It was an honor to have Coach Cox as he was an All-American at Georgia Southern and he was my coach at Cleveland Junior High School. He was a powerful encourager and was the first coach to teach me how to be a quarterback at football. He also trained me to be a punting specialist in football. As the quarterback for the Cleveland Blue Jays we were undefeated my 8th grade year. Coach Cox also coached me in basketball and our team went to the state playoffs but were beaten by Hand Jr. High School. Coach Cox said to study hard, make good school grades and the sky is the limit!

COACH BOB BELL... Bell was my Spartanburg High School football coach. He was a Marine while serving our country and you can be sure we were in superb physical condition. In October of 1965, we played a rivalry game, for the first time, between Spartanburg High and Dorman High. Coach's words still ring in my ears. At half-time he called me to the side and called me by the name my friends call me. He said, "Junior, of all your trophies and awards you have won, believe me, tonight is the only football game people will remember you for...as the Spartanburg High Crimson Tide Quarterback." When he finished saying these words my heart was set on fire to give it all I had and to go beyond the goal line. It became the greatest football game I ever played.

COACH GUS PRILL... He is one of the greatest church basketball coaches I ever played for! He instructed me, "Attend my Sunday School class two times out of each month and you can play basketball for me." I took him up on the challenge and he became a strong spiritual leader in my life. He would later get me a basketball scholarship to Presbyterian College, and like a dummy, I did not accept.

COACH BOB TALLANT... He nicknamed me "Tar Bucket" as I played center field for the Optimist baseball team. He would lead us to many city championships and guide us toward making "right decisions" in life. Tallant took me on my first vacation as a teenager. I am forever indebted to this incredible coach.

DR. FRED WOLFE... Not only a coach, but Wolfe directed my life spiritually. He taught me about the Holy Spirit and living the surrendered life. He taught me about prayer and intimacy with Jesus. For twenty-six years, and even today, he has mentored me in my walk with Jesus. To me, he is a true soldier of the cross of Jesus Christ.

DR. ROBBIE HOWARD... Always encourages me to be a relentless soul winner for Jesus. He said to me, "Memorize the words of God and speak them as you witness and watch God save souls." He and his wife, Peggy, were like my Mom and Dad when I was away from home. He treated me like a son!

DUB GRANT... This incredible man carried my name before God with tears and fasting. He invited me to church the day I met Jesus. From an alcoholic to being saved, to teaching Sunday school, and then to be called of God to preach the gospel of Jesus Christ is almost more than I can comprehend. Thank you Mr. Grant for not giving up on me!

RUPERT GUEST... Pastor Guest became my Pastor and my friend. He prayed with me to receive Jesus in 1975. He has been a partner in ministry and trained me to become a market place witness. It would be Pastor Guest who would say to me, "Dave, we need laymen on fire for Jesus who will be willing to take the gospel of Jesus to the streets to seek lost souls." He believed in me and I would not be where I am in ministry today without his training.

DR. MICHAEL HAMLET... My current pastor would play a key role in what has turned out to be my evangelistic calling in 2004. In my heart I knew beyond a shadow of a doubt God has put me in the spiritual office of an EVANGELIST. Pastor Hamlet ministered to me in difficult days and he also instructed me to pray for thirty days in seeking my new direction in ministry.

After thirty days of praying I became a broken man and through this the Lord raised me up to operate Dave Walton Evangelistic Association. Thank you Pastor Mike! I am forever indebted!

JUNIOR HILL... He calls me his South Carolina Junebug. I call him my Alabama Junebug. He is one of my greatest heroes. Together, we evangelize. He writes, "Over these many years of being a traveling preacher, I have met hundreds of men and woman with a passion to win the lost, but very, very few with the intensity of Dave Walton. He is a man on fire for Jesus! He lives and breathes soul-winning. If you want a man who will come to your church and build a fire of evangelism in your fellowship I would encourage you to invite Dave. You will be glad that you did and your church will be blessed." Evangelist Junior Hill.

BILL AMILK... Bill was a South Carolina businessman. He was my faithful prayer warrior and encouraged me to start city wide revivals. He fanned the fires of faith in my heart to seek God's plan and purpose in my ministry. At the age of seventy, Bill was promoted to Heaven, but I will never forget the impact he made on my life with his prayers. His friendship is forever branded in my heart. Bill's wife, Linda, continues to be a praying force for Dave Walton Ministries. I am very thankful.

MEET DAVE WALTON

On May 6, 1947, Alexander and Melba Lee Walton gave birth to Dave Walton. For the nine months prior to his birth, his parents referred to their baby as Junior. When he was born Alexander asked his wife if she would consider naming the baby David O'dell Walton; after his brother who died shortly after an accident on his Radio Flyer, red wagon, at the age of seven. She agreed.

Today, there is a tombstone with ***their*** name on it. He was born June 8th, 1929 and died June 26th, 1936. His parent's names were Scott and Callie Walton. Alexander had one sister, Viola. Dave likes to show the photo of his uncle's tombstone, then tell you when he was *born again*; on September 7th, 1975.

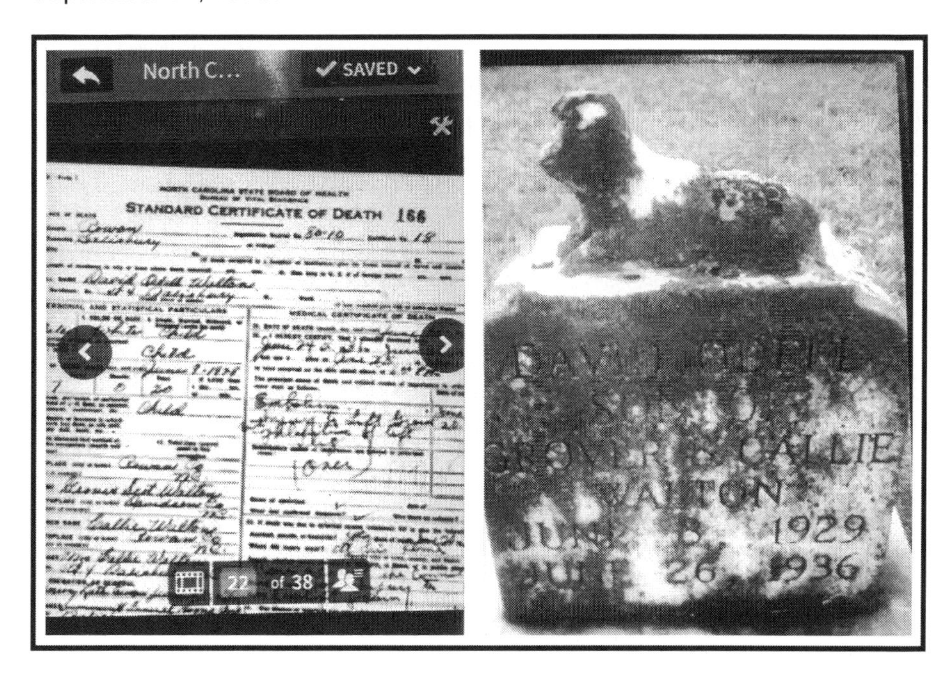

After Dave's father was promoted to Heaven, he received his Bible where he read, "Junebug, (Dave's nickname) you have carried my brother's name well." He said he could hear his father's voice clearly speaking to him, through his own tears, "Finish well and finish strong!"

Dave is the oldest of his five siblings. In order by birth are, Sue, Boyd, Stan, and Kay. Household salvation has always been a goal while ministering to individuals. Dave experienced the growth in his life because Jesus was bragged on at home and they experienced God's love, daily.

Dave graduated from Spartanburg High School, Spartanburg Junior College, and Limestone College. All parents expect greatness from their children. All parents hope to watch their children find their place and calling in this world. Every parent longs for their children to find happiness.

Each of us wanders until we find our place. Eventually the wonder happens! Dave was a teenager when his life purpose began revealing his future to both him, and everyone around him. Plans began to unfold. Lives began to be changed right before his eyes. The 'wonder' was overwhelming at times. The Walton family was not disappointed.

This book is a copulation of events. As you read, open your heart and mind. Be sure to read between the lines, for secrets are laced throughout each word. You will discover God's goodness, grace, and mercy.

The testimonials will inspire you. Many are 'thank you' notes from Dave Walton, while others will supercharge your belief system as you meet God. Be prepared to challenge yourself as you are stirred to evangelize.

As you take this journey, recall the miracles you have experienced in your life. You will find them a pure inspiration, where you may have overlooked the hand of God during the experience.

Today, as was then, is the day of salvation. It is never too late to thank Him, praise Him, allow Him to stir up your faith, and show you His next plan. It is in front of you. Seek His face. After salvation, there is always more hope past the goal line.

Serving Him,

Evangelist Vickie Hodge Holt,
Editor/Publisher

PAST THE GOAL LINE

In 1972, I graduated from Limestone College and in September of 1972, I applied for work at the Regency Health Spa, located in the Pinewood Shopping Center. I got the job and would later be promoted to club manager in 1973. The Spa consisted of weight lifting machines, arm curl machines, tread mills, and much more to help people get their bodies in shape.

I remember one year we were on a membership drive and we contacted Dennis Tinerino, an American bodybuilder who held records as a four-time Mr. Universe, Mr. America, and Hall of Famer. He put on a show like no one else and we broke records on membership enrollment that day. Dennis and I became friends and stayed in touch for a long time.

We also had Lee Haney work out at our Spa for a short time. Lee shares the all-time record for Mr. Olympia titles at eight with Ronnie Coleman. Lee Haney is my favorite pro bodybuilder and a legend in his own right.

I really enjoyed this type of work because I was helping people get their bodies in better shape, thus producing a better lifestyle physically and emotionally. In 1975, a man came to join our Spa by the name of Mr. Dub Grant, and I was to introduce him to his workout and help him get in shape. Well, I worked him out like a rented mule and then I discovered he was sixty-two years old.

Dub was a great gentleman and in our conversation, he stated he knew me from my football days as a quarterback at Spartanburg High School Crimson Tide. He nearly recalled the entire 1965 game play by play! I was truly amazed at his memory. He closed his remarks by stating, “I saw the 64 yard run you had in that game, which beat the opposing team.” He then asked me to have lunch with him. I accepted. We became friends and he would often take me out for a meal. I later discovered that he knew of my Daddy’s boxing career. We had long talks about football and boxing and I grew very fond Mr. Grant.

He continued coming to the Spa for a long period of time and then one day he left the Spa and I did not see him again. Some thirty days passed and one evening I received a phone call from Mr. Grant asking me to do him a favor; of which I agreed. Later I learned the favor was to go to church with him the coming Sunday morning. I agreed to go with him but I was in high hopes I could meet him at the church he invited me to go to so if I decided to change my mind I could make up some off-the-wall excuse for not making it there.

Mr. Grant said, “No way. I am coming to pick you up and we will go together.” I think Mr. Grant had a plan and was working it out! I went to church with him on September 7, 1975, to Arch Street Baptist Church, and as they say, the rest is history; His story…in me. My life was changed forever because of Jesus Christ.

You would think my getting saved would be enough for Mr. Grant, but that was not the case. In January of 1976, I was scheduled to speak at our church on what is called Men’s Day, and Mr. Grant purposed we advertise the meeting. I strongly disagreed. Mr. Grant won out, stating that many of my friends would come to see if this is real and that I would have a chance to introduce them to Jesus. I was thinking, ‘this is unbelievable, because I think he is trying to make a preacher out of me and that is not going happen!’

Well, the next day came, and it was time for me to preach my first sermon. I had studied hard and felt prepared. Pastor said I had thirty minutes to preach my message and I thought that was just not enough time.

My first sermon lasted about seven minutes. I preached all I knew about the Bible and said to myself, “That is it and I am done with preaching!” It is amazing how God works! It took until 1983 before I would accept the call to preach God’s Word. Somehow I believe Mr. Grant and my Grandmother, who are in Heaven, were working out God’s plan for my life. I am forever grateful. I am truly living the God miracle, everyday!

Dave's Father, Alexander Walton, was inducted into the Boxing Hall of Fame in 2012.

CAROLINAS BOXING  HALL OF FAME

2012 Hall of Fame Inductee

Alexander Walton
AKA "Buck Earnhardt" *(Deceased)*

Wife: Melba Lee Walton of Spartanburg, SC

Personal Data: Born: July 7, 1926 in Salisbury, NC, the son of Geroge and Callie (Waller) Walton; raised by his aunt and uncle, Mr. & Mrs. T. C. Earnhardt.

Children: Five children - 3 Boys, 2 Girls, 10 Grandchildren and 8 Great-Grandchildren

Hobbies: Coaching

Buck enlisted in United States Navy on March 9, 1944. On August 31, 1944 he is listed on board the USS Clyde. Then on April 1, 1946 he is listed among the crew of the USS Unicoi as a Seaman 1st Class. Buck began his boxing career during his service in the Navy.

Many of the results were not available. During this period of time, the newspapers focused on the War both in Europe and Pacific. Sports pages in the Spartanburg newspapers were usually one-page and devoted mostly to baseball.

An article titled "Carl Chastain Heads Armory Fight Card Here - Boxes Buck Earnhardt in 10-Rounder" which appeared in the Spartanburg Herald Journal, state: **"Buck Earnhardt has 40 triumphs, 21 setbacks and a pair of draws. He has floored 28 foes."**

Former boxers from this era estimate that Buck probably had about 100 professional fights. By 1957, Buck had been boxing for over 10 years.

Awards: Buck coached with Henry "Pappy" Gault for the city of Spartanburg Boxing Team in the mid 1960's.

In 1963, Buck coached the Salvation Army Boys' Club Bantam League Football team to the city championship with an 8-0 record.

In 1964, Buck's Little League Baseball team the "Luncheon Optimist", posted a perfect 22-0 record to win the city championship.

Several players from these teams went on to

play college ball, with one player from this championship baseball team going on to play professional baseball.

Buck influenced a lot of young men's lives in the Spartan Mills community in and out of the ring.

He retired from Southern Railway in 1990 after 40 years of service.

He passed in Spartanburg on September 29, 1994.

- 9 -

July 6, 1957. Photo on the left was in the Spartanburg Journal.

Photo on the right is Alexander "Buck" Walton.

Alexander used the name Buck Earnhart as his boxing career name.

When Alexander Walton was about twelve years old he traveled from the family home in Salisbury North Carolina to live with relatives, the Earnharts, who lived on Arch Street in the Spartan Mill Village area of Spartanburg South Carolina.

Also see page 124 for more on the induction into the Hall of Fame.

Earnhart And Chastain Battle To Draw Again

By SONNY SMITH
Herald Sports Writer

Buck Earnhart and Carl Chastain left the way open for another meeting in their grudge series as they battled to a 10-round deadlock last night at the Spartanburg Armory before [illegible] fight fans.

This draw was the second between the pair along with a decision in ten-rounds by the Asheville, N. C. native Chastain.

No knockdowns were registered during the bout although each fighter went to his knees once as the result of a slip. Both boxers displayed a willingness to mix it up during the evening much to the delight of the crowd.

In the final round, the two started firing away from long-range to gain a knockout. But the big blows were either off the mark or blocked.

The final summary went: Judge [illegible] 4-4 and two even and Referee Guard Wyatt and Judge Strahan, 3-3 and four even.

"Battlin'" Buck jumped the gun in the opening round eager to avenge his defeat at the hands of Chastain. During the sizing up round, he landed a solid left hook to Chastain's side. Chastain, the [illegible], found the range in the second with some nifty lefts and a combination volley to the body. Earnhart pounded him with several right hand shots at the bell.

The first blood of the night appeared in the third round when Earnhart drew a crimson stream from Chastain's nose. Throughout the remainder of the fight, Earnhart found his beak a tender spot for anything from blows to elbows.

Round three was one of the best Earnhart recorded.

Again in the fourth Earnhart proved the aggressor with a flicking left and rights to the head. At the bell, Earnhart had Chastain on the ropes.

Chastain picked up the tempo in rounds five and six with a sparkling counterattack. But his dripping nose continued to plague him. The seventh was a lively round with toe-to-toe slugging the whole time. Rounds eight and nine were alike in nature to the seventh with a crowd pleasing slugging exhibition.

In the opening match of the night, [illegible] Byrd racked up a four-round decision over fellow Spartan George Johnson in a middleweight event.

Johnny Kilpatrick, a stylish middleweight from Asheville, scored a fourth round technical knockout over Spartanburg's Olin Rice. The time was 1:48. Rice gained an early edge over Kilpatrick, but in the fourth round Rice, the hunter during the opening rounds, became the hunted as Kilpatrick stalked him around the ring.

Spartanburg amateur Buster Edwards decisioned Jerry Staton of Hendersonville, N. C., in a simon-pure bout between a pair of light heavyweights.

Two of the bouts including the eight-round semifinal between Spartanburg's Charlie Porter and Sam Free of Hendersonville were cancelled.

FROWNING BLOW . . . Buck Earnhart, left, sticks a looping left jab into the face of Carl Chastain of Asheville, N.C., in the third round of their ten-round lightweight bout last night at the Spartanburg Armory. The two slugged it out to the second draw in their three meetings. (Photo by B&B Studio.)

Buck Earnhart right, slugged it out in 10 rounds with Carl Chastain.

Earnhart had Chastain on the ropes.

Fight Lineup

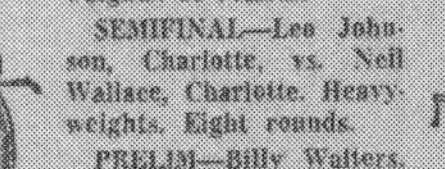

MAIN EVENT — Robert Oliphant, Charlotte, vs. Jim Kelly, Charlotte. Welterweights. 10 rounds.

SEMIFINAL—Leo Johnson, Charlotte, vs. Neil Wallace, Charlotte. Heavyweights. Eight rounds.

PRELIM—Billy Walters, Rock Hill, S. C., vs. John May, Charlotte. Heavyweights. Six rounds.

PRELIM — Buck Earnhardt, Spartanburg, S. C., vs. Carl Chasteen, Brevard. Welterweights. Six rounds.

Dave's Treasured Handwritten Note from His Mother.
Dated March 12, 1986.

March 12
Wed Night
1986

Junior,

I watched Battle Cry tonight and I want you to know how very much I Love you. I never was good at putting my feelings into words.

I wanted to do so much for you, It hurt me deeply when you had to do without things.

I know if we had been blessed with money all of my children would have been spoiled brats. I would have given you everything you wanted.

God always knows best. I'm so happy He gave me a son like you instead of wealth.

I Praise God that you belong to Him and you're not ashamed of the Name of Jesus, that you care about and love the unlovely as Jesus did.

I usually destroy things like this that unveils my heart, but something told me to send it to you. May you walk in his footsteps forever.

All My Love
Mama

TESTIMONY OF DAVE WALTON

Scott & Cally "Sis" Walton

As a young teenager my life was wrapped around sports. I practiced hard and wanted to be a winner. I played on several championship teams in baseball, football, and basketball.

My father worked with Southern Railway for forty-two years and also fought professionally as a prize fighter. Daddy compiled 62 fights, winning 48, and 28 of those were won by KO (knockouts). Yet out of all the things Mom and Dad ever did for me, I treasure the time they spent with me at ballgames. Their presence made it awesome! I can still hear my Daddy screaming at the top of his lungs, while I was at bat, "Keep your eyes on the ball. You can hit him!" It seems only like yesterday...oh, how time flies.

I remember Grandma Sis coming to visit us the summer I graduated from high school. I showed her my picture and name in the sports page of the local paper. I can hear her say, "I am so proud of you, Dave, but I will be even happier when you name is written in the Lamb's Book of Life." I loved Grandma but religion set on the bench in my life. My coach's sermons were more of an inspiration then than any sermon I had heard in church.

Off I went, focused, determined, with the eye of the tiger to make a name for myself in the sports arena. I was gathering trophies and letter jackets from Cleveland Junior High. The late Spartanburg Journal sports editor Ed McGrath, on Monday, February 19, 1962, wrote of our state bound championship team, "the classiest performer of them all is eighth grade ball-handler Junior Walton."

Our team had gone to the state finals in basketball. We had gone undefeated in football. I had been named to the All Star Basketball team. In the back of my mind, I had always dreamed of being a champion like my Daddy. I pressed even harder in my workouts; pushing myself day after day to be the best I could be. I wanted my Daddy to be proud of me.

I made the starting line-up in baseball with the Spartanburg High Red Birds while still at Cleveland Junior High. I lettered that year and made the triple "A" all-star team. I was on cloud nine and felt that my life was in order.

I became the QUARTERBACK for the SPARTANBURG HIGH CRIMSON TIDE. I was known as Junior Walton, the gritty little SHS Crimson Tide Quarterback.

And...then it happened! My world began to fall apart. I did something I said I would never do. I broke my Mom and Dad's heart. I brought shame to my parents and entire family. The scouts quit watching me. My double life was catching up to me. I was living a lie.

I graduated from high school and had a two-year scholarship to a small college to play football. Instead, I walked off the field and told my parents and friends that life didn't matter. I knew I was lying. My parents were deeply hurt and broken hearted. To add insult to injury, they discovered my horrible alcohol problem.

If my parents were disappointed, I was even more down about the turn that my life had taken. I WAS TRAPPED! I lived in bars. I gambled. I would leave bars broken and ashamed. Weekend and after weekend was the same in my life. I was held captive by alcohol for years.

I really wanted to change my lifestyle, but I didn't know how. I was feeling hopeless, in a rut, bound about this thing called social or moderate drinking. In 1969 I married Diane Reeves. We had a daughter we named Holly and I was filled with joy, and hope that this could make a real change in my life.

I was wrong!

In 1975, I met a man by the name of Dub Grant. He built a friendship with me and soon invited me to church. What I did not know was that Mr. Grant had been fasting and praying for me for many days and nights. We arrived late at the church and I tried to find a place to hide from among the congregation. The only place available was the third pew from the front. There is where I heard Pastor Rupert preach the word of God. He said that the God of the Bible could set an alcoholic FREE. I became convicted and was ashamed of my lifestyle. I went forward and received Jesus as my Lord and Savior. I later learned that my younger brother had meet Jesus and he and Mr. Grant had invited the Walton family to church on this day!

—Photo by B&B Studio

Spartan High Awards Winners

These six outstanding Spartanburg High athletes were honored at the annual Spring Sports Banquet as the Most Valuable Players in their sport. From left: Larry Linder, tennis; Rusty Applegate, golf; Ray Adams, track and Outstanding Spring Sports Athlete; Todd McKay, swimming; Ted Phelps, baseball; Junior Walton, [illegible] batting champion (.357).

Outstanding Spring Sports Athlete

"Junior" Walton

Baseball Batting Champion

KAY WALTON WALDEN'S POEM ABOUT DAVE

A BROTHER'S LOVE

You prayed for me seven long years
You sacrificed your time and your tears.
Your main concern was for my very soul
Knowing that my salvation would be the final goal.
You taught me that "love" never gives up
You cared enough to take my cup.
I know that it was your love and prayers that carried me through
So many times in my life I didn't know where to turn or what to do.
Lord, show him how much I love him, how much I care
I'll forever be grateful for his love and his prayers.
I've always been proud to say you're my brother and my friend
This poem is to let you know, **I LOVE YOU!**, just had to say it again.
Show me Lord how to love and not give up
Give me "Total Commitment" as my cup
So that I might be an intercessor for my brother and his heavy heart
Let me pray that joy will return, complete in every part
I pray for a miracle Lord, this is serious business
Open up the heavens for Downtown Rescue Mission!
Let the people marvel at what can be done
When we put it in the hands of Jesus, God's only Son.

AMEN

KAY W. Walden
December 7, 1989

You have been such an inspiration to me in your walk with the Lord I just wanted to say "thank you" again for all you've done for me and for caring when I felt no one else did.

TESTIMONIALS

“Bragging on Jesus”

Don Stanley

Proverbs 18: 24 A man that hath friends must shew himself friendly: and there is a friend that sticketh closer than a brother.

I want to introduce you to my friend Don Stanley. We grew up together in Spartan Mill on Arch Street. We have been friends for some sixty years. He is the kind of friend who tells you something and you can take it to the bank. Don and I played football, baseball, and basketball together from the little leagues, American Legion, into middle school, and through to graduation at Spartanburg High School. Don was an incredible athlete and a superstar in baseball. He won scholarships to the University of South Carolina in baseball and his academics set him on pace to become a pharmacist.

I would not be here, in ministry, had it not been for Don Stanley. We traveled across America sharing Jesus in churches, prisons, schools, football stadiums and in the streets of America. We were called into ministry in 1983 and the Lord would open doors in some 500 churches over a twenty-year period to preach the gospel of Jesus.

Don Stanley's prison testimony touched thousands of lives and I am a witness of seeing over 100,000 people receive Jesus from his fiery, passionate preaching. He shared his testimony on the 700 Club, Oral Roberts Show, and the TBN Networks; and many other shows followed.

God poured out His blessing on us as we traveled America "bragging on Jesus."

Thank you, Don Stanley, for your friendship and solid commitment to the "Cross of Jesus Christ." You are truly a TOTAL MAN of GOD! Our ministry was truly a SUPERNATURAL MINISTRY.

IT'S SUPERNATURAL

We were in a supernatural revival meeting in the Mullins and Marion area of South Carolina. The four-day revival turned into a thirteen days of revival meetings. We had to move the meeting to the Marion High School to accommodate the crowds. I had to return to Spartanburg South Carolina for a mission board meeting and when the meeting ended, I asked one of the pastors, "How do you know when to close and revival when so many people are being saved"?

The pastor said, "Always leave the revival on a high note." Well, that did not quite answer my question, but I had something to think about on my flight back to the revival.

While in prayer, I was overtaken with the presence of God in my heart. I heard him say, "Philip left a great revival in Samaria to meet one man." I remember the story well. The Evangelist met with the Ethiopian eunuch, in the book of Acts. The meeting took place in the desert. My heart was stirred and I was sure that God was going to stop the revival and we would go the next meeting and meet someone important. On Friday the pastor of the church came and met with me and Don Stanley and said he believed Friday would be the final night of revival. My heart leapt because I knew the LORD was doing something SUPERNATURAL. The revival ended with hundreds coming to Christ and we departed to the next meeting in Rock Hill, South Carolina.

We were involved with a simultaneous revival meeting throughout Rock Hill. On Monday, we had a gathering of preachers, pastors, evangelists and leaders of the local churches. The man in charge asked if anyone had any great news to share about things God was doing in ministry. Well, we testified of the many souls saved in the Mullins area. All of a sudden one man on the front row of the church dove out face down and was praying. He rose up and came to speak to us. He introduced himself as Brother Fred. We did not know him, but others soon let us know of the mighty man of God. He was in the church in Mobile, Alabama. God whispered in my heart, "He is the man."

He would meet with us in our hotel room and invite us for a revival at Cottage Hill Baptist Church in Mobile, Alabama. He would later invite us to the Pastors' Conference of Alabama with several thousand pastors in attendance. Don would give his testimony and the fire of the Lord fell! It was supernatural as pastors began to schedule us for revival meetings.

For fifteen years we preached in Alabama revivals.

It is the work of God! It is His divine leadership and He poured out His favor on us. I don't know what you are facing now, but I know a God who is able to do mighty things in your life. Yield to HIM! Call on Him! He is near and wants to fill you with His grace and mercy and incredible forgiveness. Let Him be SUPERNATURAL in your life.

FRED H. WOLFE, PASTOR

SUNDAY, AUG. 10, 1986

Cottage Hill Baptist Church

The message I brought this past Sunday entitled, "Is There Anything I Can Do For You", is one that I want you to ask God to let you live out in your life day by day. As we walk in love, we will see God's power and glory manifested in this body. We need to constantly have our spiritual eyes and physical eyes open for those around us that are hurting and are needy and we need to selflessly love them and minister to them. We are one in Christ; when a brother hurts, we hurt. When another rejoices, we rejoice.

I'm looking forward to great services Sunday. A few months ago when I was in South Carolina at the revival at my mother's church, I met two laymen who are absolutely on fire for God. Dave Walton and Don Stanley remind me so much of Arthur Blessitt. Don Stanley was saved in prison about three years ago. Since his release, he has been mightily used of God all across South Carolina, North Carolina, and Georgia. He and Dave Walton have started a ministry to the poor in Spartanburg, South Carolina that is being greatly used of God to influence that city. As I heard Don Stanley's testimony, I not only felt impressed to ask him to give it in our church but to give it for the Alabama Baptist Pastors' Conference on November 17. So, in this Sunday morning services, Don Stanley and Dave Walton will be sharing with us. Folks, you don't want to miss this. They ministered to me as few people have ever done. Don will be giving his testimony Sunday morning and Dave will be praying. Then Sunday night, they are going to lead us in a great worship service together. God is literally using them to bring thousands of souls to Jesus. They have a tremendous influence and impact on young people. Do not miss this Sunday! I will be here. I know I will be blessed and I'm looking forward to seeing you.

Jesus is Lord! Bro. Fred

Brother Fred Wolfe's letter dated August 10, 1986.

Jesus Is Lord

Dave,

You are truly a man of God! a dear friend and brother you have my love and prayers - Finish strong and finish well!

Jesus Is Lord!

Fred K Wolfe

PASTOR RUPERT GUEST

I met Dave Walton in 1975 when he joined Arch Street Baptist Church. He immediately began working in various programs of the church showing great interest in outreach and witnessing. He took Jesus to heart in Mark 8: 38 and the apostle Paul who said in Romans 1: 16, “I am not ashamed of the gospel of Christ.” Wherever Dave goes, in grocery stores, pharmacies, doctor offices, restaurants, or on the streets, he talks to people about Jesus.

In 1980 Dave went with me to Haiti on a mission trip. His love for lost people intensified, especially for youth. God has given him the opportunity to preach to young people in schools across the country where hundreds have come to Christ. God has also extended his ministry to Nicaragua where he builds homes, digs wells, and holds crusade meetings.

In summary, Dave is a close friend and brother in Christ. In my 87 years of life, I have never known a greater soul winner. Enjoy reading his book!

God bless,
Rupert

WALTON WYATT

My grandfather, Dave Walton, taught me at a very young age to spread the Word of God. It didn’t matter where we were he always had us spreading spiritual tracks or just going up to a people to share our story. I remember one specific time which was not too long ago. We were getting my oil changed and there stood a man who seemed to be angered at something. So, my grandpa started talking to him and it ended up he was a preacher himself. It made him change his whole attitude, at once! I thought that was amazing! I honestly do believe my grandfather has led a person to Christ in every fast food restaurant he has been in. And, it’s no doubt he’s got the power of God down in his soul.

DEPRESSED

I read the scriptures, and I see God rescuing David time and time again. David's heart was always turned toward God in good times and bad times. Have you ever felt that everyone was against your or just did not understand what you were going through? This causes great pain to the one living in the dark days.

I have been there, in the pit for days, where I cried out night after night and no one came to my rescue. Alone and depressed by circumstances beyond my control, I felt like giving up...and a knock came to the door, but I had no strength to get up and see who it was. Diane went to the door and it was Mom and two sisters. As my wife says, "They had fire in their eyes and they were on a mission from God!"

They sat me in a chair and circled me, praying, and I mean PRAYING! For thirty minutes they spoke scripture over me and cried out to the LIVING GOD to deliver me. I can't say that I had a great vision, a powerful deliverance and jumped up and shouted glory, but something happened! It was as if the atmosphere changed. What I could not do for myself, God sent my Mom and two sisters to cry out for me, through their prayers.

The next day I began to sense a change in my thinking and a renewed strength coming from within. Several days later, I noticed a complete change in my spiritual thinking and my physical endurance. Call it what you will, but God heard their prayer and sent deliverance to my life. I am forever grateful for their boldness and tender hearts to come and pray for me. I am not totally sure, but I believe God was allowing me to go through something and the result would be that I would turn my heart totally to trust Him in all things. Somehow I believe I died that day as my life seed fell to the ground and would later bring forth much fruit for the kingdom of God. I learned that I can do nothing outside of Jesus Christ. It is not I but Christ who leads me and directs me in my earthly assignments. To GOD be all the glory!

Psalm 50:15 And call upon me in the day of trouble: I will deliver thee, and thou shalt glorify me.

MY FAILURES

"Give me the ball, Coach!" It is 1962 and we are playing Chapman Jayvees and they had beaten the socks off of us in an earlier basketball game, but our team had grown in unity and we believed we could win. It was a hard fought game between Cleveland Junior High and Chapman. Everyone was playing with all the energy they could muster. We were down to a few seconds on the clock and we were being beaten by one point.

Coach Gilbert Cox called time out and we made a huddle around him to discuss the strategies of the final seconds.

Coach looked me dead in the eye and said, "Walton, shoot the ball and make it!"

The horn sounded and we hit the basketball court. An in- bound pass was thrown to me. I turned and made the shot. A high arching shot was on its way to the basket as the buzzer sounded to end the game. I heard it, "SWISH," and there is no greater sound in basketball than the swish of the net. We won 41-40!

Last year we were city champions and went to the state finals, but this year, we had struggled to win a game. To tell the truth, I have had more defeats and failures than victories. I have learned to be thankful and appreciate all of life's failures. They have been great teachers.

Defeats have taught me to never give up. In my heart I must try again and again with an attitude of never giving up or quitting. I apply this to my life when it comes to soul winning. I have learned that rejection to the gospel comes more than accepting the gospel. In my earlier days of witnessing in the marketplace, I would become very discouraged until a wiser man said, "You cannot fail at soul winning. God only asks you to share your faith and leave the increase to Him." Those words set me free! My attitude totally changed about witnessing. I somewhat understand now what Jesus said, "Follow Me and I will make you a Fisher of Men." God does it!

HE HEARD MY CRY

The idea that an evangelist doesn't have fear or problems is nonsense. We struggle like everyone else and we have some of the darkest days one would ever face.

At Jesus' death His disciples were scattered, and fear ruled their lives. It would be after the resurrection of Jesus from the dead that this would change. They were locked up in a room and Jesus came walking through the locked door and shortly after this, their fear left them. Jesus has a way of destroying fear!

Even as an evangelist, I have faced that thing called fear. At times it has paralyzed me and kept me up all night, believing for the worst. O, how I have cried out many times for help to fight off fear; until...this powerful encounter took place one night in my home.

My wife Diane and I were facing some big mountains in our lives and we were helpless with no answer in sight. I could not find sleep. Around 2 am I got up to pray and read my Bible. All of sudden fear grabbed me and I could hardly breathe. I was being tormented. I cried out passionately, out of control, with a loud voice, asking God to help me.

Suddenly, my room where I was praying, was filled with His presence. I heard within my heart, "Fear Not, I am the Lion of the tribe of Judah."

With a loud roar the voice continued and said, "I am at your side."

Fear left and God poured His fire in and through me. I give Him praise!

2 Timothy 1: 7 For God hath not given us the spirit of fear: but of power, and love, and of a sound body.

SEPTEMBER 7, 1975

Upon receiving Jesus Christ as my Savior on this date, my life was turned right side up. I remember reading the Bible and this verse leaping off the pages into my heart. Matthew 4: 19 says, "Follow me, and I will make you a fisher of men." I have done some fishing in my life and enjoyed it, but here Jesus spoke of fishing for people. I was not sure how, but I knew Jesus wanted me to share my story of salvation and I just knew some folks would repent of their sins and pray for Jesus to come into their lives just like I did.

Another verse in Jeremiah set my heart ablaze about fishing for souls. Jeremiah 5:14, "Wherefore thus saith the Lord God of Hosts, because you speak this word, behold, I will make my words in thy mouth fire, and this people wood, and it shall devour them." It was like the Lord let me see that if I used His Word when speaking to people about Jesus and His love and forgiveness of sin, that God would put fire on my words.

As I memorized scripture and used it in testifying, I saw people-out of nowhere-start crying, while others hung their heads in shame. It became apparent to me that God's Word is alive and if I would use it, God would make me a "fishers of men".

I guess the hardest thing I had to watch for was picking the fruit before its time. I have learned to listen to the Holy Spirit so that I can recognize when it is planting season, watering time, and time to harvest. God alone is the only One who can harvest and we are to pray for the Lord of the harvest to send forth laborers into the fields to reap the harvest.

I remember testifying to a man who was a church member and when I asked him to share his story of salvation he said, "I have never run around on my wife. I have never killed anyone. I go to church every Sunday and I am doing the best I can at being good so God will accept me."

Forty-five minutes later the Lord opened his heart to see that he needed Jesus and his sins needed to be cast as far as the East is to the West. Jerry finally saw the Light and his life quickly changed.

I'm glad I went that day to testify about Jesus, because a year later, Jerry died, unexpectedly.

On another occasion, I was made aware of a man who was very sick with cancer. His concerned friends asked me to go and see if his name was written in Heaven. I had a string of revivals and just forgot about this man. Finally, I arrived in Spartanburg and was driving home when all of a sudden this strong desire came over me to visit this man in the hospital. Isaiah 30:21 speaks of a voice behind you saying, "...this is the way."

It happened! I went straight to the hospital.

When I arrived at the door of the room number where he was hospitalized, to my amazement, there were no visitors. As I stepped into the room I heard him say, "I've been expecting you." He went on to say that as a child he was baptized and joined a church, but by his own words he said, "I am not saved." He said, "God has sent you to make sure my name is written in Heaven." It was a powerful God moment as he prayed to be forgiven of his sins and to invite Jesus into his heart. Two months later this special friend died. I know he is in Heaven. Thank you Jesus!

I have spent my Christian life telling others about the saving grace of the Lord Jesus. In every country, He has opened the door for me to do mission work He gave me souls for my labor. He is faithful and He wants all of us to be fishers of men.

My fishing for souls, under the leadership o the Holy Spirit, has taken me to prisons in Nicaragua, South Africa, America, and schools and churches both in America and Nicaragua. It is incredible how the Lord has opened doors for me to brag on Jesus. Football teams and the FCA events held in schools listen to me brag on Him. In the market place and my sphere of influence, the Lord sets up divine appointments for me to testify of His great love for people.

Open your heart and ask the Lord to baptize you in a fresh fire of soul winning. Remember...there is a Heaven and there is a place named Hell. We should be telling everyone about both. Will you decide to go fishing and make an eternal difference in someone's life?

HAITI 1980

My first mission trip outside the United States was to Haiti in 1980 with Evangelist John Tierney. He conducted a revival at our church in Spartanburg, South Carolina. As an evangelist who preached all across America, he also became a church planter. He founded orphanages and schools and supported feeding children in Haiti. His love for soul winning touched my life. This is one mission trip that would change my life forever. I had never experienced, seeing first hand, little children starving. It broke my heart.

One afternoon we took several hundred pounds of rice to a poor community. They came with pots, bags, bottles, and some ladies used their dress to form a scoop in order to hold the rice. As the line dwindled I looked at the ground and noticed there was not a grain of rice on the ground. No waste, whatsoever.

One night, while on this mission trip, I heard a strong cry from outside our mission camp. I asked the evangelist what was going on. With sad eyes and broken speech he said a mother is crying because her child has died. He left and went to the place where the child lay and ministered to the mother.

Later I met a young man by the name of Jean Paul Fritz who was sixteen years old. He was taking care of his sister because his mother and father had passed away. I went to his home, which was a shack. It was clean. He showed me pictures of their parents. It was a moving experience. I asked young Fritz what I could do for him, and he said, "I need to get an education so I can better myself." I agreed, so we worked with his pastor Juan Paul Edmonds to secure him a spot for education in the church school system.

This mission trip is forever embedded in my heart and I still think about it today, some thirty-six years later. I would encourage you, the reader, to go on a mission trip somewhere out of this country and experience how blessed we are to live in a free country. Others are much more unfortunate. One tremendous ministry I would recommend is Chosen Children Ministries located in Spartanburg, South Carolina. Travel with them into Nicaragua and you will never be the same!

GRAND BAY, ALABAMA

Don Stanley and I went to Grand Bay, Alabama on August 16, 1987 to preach in a revival at Friendship Baptist Church for Dr. Robbie Howard. He is a fireball preacher and he opened the door for us to preach. He had prepared his people in the secret place of prayer and the expectation of souls to be saved was high. The gospel music during the revival was electrifying and the people were praising God. He did not disappoint them. God came down and met with us.

It was a "barn burner" revival with over three hundred souls saved! The crowds were so large the sanctuary could not hold them. They set up cameras in the gym for the overflow. The community wanted to be a part of this incredible revival.

This time together forged a great friendship with Dr. Robbie and Peggy Howard. We scheduled more revivals in the future. Brother Robbie said, "When I heard the testimony of Don Stanley at the Pastors' Conference at Cottage Hill, I knew this duo team would be at my church as soon as they had an open date."

It is hard to describe the love we have for this God fearing preacher and his wife. Robbie, a powerful preacher and soul winner and Peggy a prayer warrior, and might I add, an awesome cook. These two servants of God would help us through difficult times in ministry and our love for them is deep. They have since gone to Heaven and we miss them and their spiritual advice.

TIRE TROUBLE AND A FIFTEEN DOLLAR TESTIMONY

In Nicaragua, you must always remain flexible when it comes to time. Our mission team was ready to go and ministry in one of the poor communities. As we were leaving the ministry compound, Carolos said, "We need to go by the tire repair shop and have our right rear tire checked. I believe we have a slow leak."

Upon arrival at the tire store, workers began looking for the leak. I was standing outside the van and began to pray for an open door to share my salvation story with these workers. Four men were working hard with air guns that were so loud you could hardly hear yourself think. They found the problem and fixed it. At that moment, the Lord stirred my heart to speak to Carlos. He in turn asked the owner if I could share my story with his workers. I told Carlos to tell the owner I would add fifteen dollars more to the bill. When the owner received this offer, he agreed to let me testify. (Fifteen dollars is about three day's wages for one employee.)

He gathered his men together in a semi-circle and the revival meeting began. The owner and all four workers and our mission team listened as I started bragging on Jesus! Four men prayed to receive Jesus and one man was so moved he began to testify of the greatness of God. He said he left his wife and children for twenty years because of the abuse of drugs and alcohol, and at the point of death and giving up on life, God came to him and saved his soul. He went on to say he went back to see if his wife would take him back and she said I have been praying for your return and God has answered my prayers.

We started praising God and shouting the victory that we were blessed with tire trouble because God brought us to a place to see people saved and to hear this man's awesome testimony.

God is alive and well! God is changing lives everywhere and it was surely a God moment at the tire store in Nicaragua.

Thank you Jesus!

SOUTH AFRICA

For thirty-seven years I have burned with an inner flame to share the gospel of Jesus Christ. I really cannot explain it, but it is with me every day of my life. I hear the cry of the hurting mother, the hungry child desiring food, and the father who is brokenhearted. I have preached in a prison in Nicaragua, in South Africa as well as in America. I have stood between the guards and shared the gospel of Jesus and seen the power of God change hardened hearts. I have been locked inside a prison with seventy-six prisoners who lived like animals and preached the gospel where I saw twenty-seven lives changed.

I know a man who cried out for Jesus behind prison bars and God set him free and called him to preach the gospel. After his release, God called him to go back to the prisons and preach to the captive and share his testimony that prisoners can be free when they come to Jesus. The real salvation experience reaches those in prison within their hearts, because we serve a mighty God!

In Nicaragua, the people are starving for the gospel. The spirit of religion has destroyed many, but God is on the scene and many souls are crying out to Jesus. I have traveled down many dusty roads to areas of Nicaragua where no churches exist. Upon seeing the spiritual starvation I have cried myself to sleep praying for God to show me a way to help build churches so that the people could be brought out of darkness into the marvelous light of Jesus.

God helped me partner with Chosen Children Ministries to build churches in Nicaragua. It has been an incredible journey. I preached under stick-built churches and saw the glory of God come down and revival break out. The lives God changed he called into ministry. I witnessed brush arbor churches grow into 200-300 membership churches in Nicaragua. God is on the move and we need to heed the call of God when He calls us in our own lives.

NICARAGUA

I fell on my knees and cried out for the lady prisoners in South Africa as I preached the love of God to them. Each lady was in prison for murder. That day God showed up in His grace and mercy and changed many lives. The prison guard who stood by my side received Jesus!

SOUTH AFRICA WOMENS PRISON

While we were in Nicaragua, I met Pastor Rito from the Leon area. WOW! He is a preaching machine! The power of God is on him and his church is on fire for the Lord. We are planning on conducting a citywide crusade in his area in July. God continues to open doors so we can brag on Jesus. I am most thankful!

DAVE AND DIANE MINISTERING IN NICARAGAU.

I pray that this year has brought you to a place in your spiritual life to become a "Son of Thunder", sounding the message of Jesus. I never get tired of telling the story of Jesus and how He saved me, to people in the marketplace. I pray that the Lord will help us reshape the human landscape and change the destiny of this generation. Could it be that the fire of the spirit that is shut up in your bones, is being called forth to produce a mighty revival in your church. If there was ever a time of destiny before us, it is now. In the heart of every great revival or awakening is the spirit of prayer. Together let's step up to the line and get started praying. Real praying, tear praying, passionate praying for God to give us a personal visitation in our services. Oh that we would have a personal encounter with the living God. Please join me in this pursuit of revival. Thank you.

Boyd Walton's dream comes true. He waited for one year to return to Nicaragua to build a home for Eric and his family. Eric's home had roof leaks and other problems. Rather than patch up the problems, Boyd surprised him by showing up with a team of construction workers and built Eric and family a new home.

UPDATE on REVIVAL

Nicaragua was invaded by 19 team members who wanted to make a difference for the hurting in Nicaragua. A City Wide Crusade and street witnessing saw the LORD save 123 Nicaraguans. Over 1200 meals served at crusade and a home was built for a poor family. The REVIVAL train rolled into Brevard,NC with Pastor Terry Whitesides at Crossroads Baptist and it was God awesome. Mitch and Suzanne Gault of "Shoes for Sharing" provided shoes for the back to school bash. The church provided music, food, clothes, and many bags of gifts. The gospel was preached and 26 souls were saved. Praise God!!!Ben Avon Baptist saw a great move of God as 25 decisions were made for Jesus. Pastor King said, I have never seen this in my 8 years of being a pastor here at Ben Avon Baptist. God deserves all the praise!

Revival train rolled into Sylvania Baptist, Al with Pastor David Starling. We met in 1988 at Henagar Baptist where a great revival broke out and several 100 people were saved. David's son and youth director introduced me to Color Wars. Youth came from many churches and I believe some 325 came aboard the revival train. It was an incredible event with 115 decisions for Christ. On to speak to Plainview , Fyffe, and Sylvania footballs teams and 42 football players prayed to receive Jesus. FCA meeting was held at Sylvania GYM and I was ask to speak to them and the LORD saved 19 students. On to David Street Baptist at a Back Pack Event and special music and free food, free back packs for students and we saw the LORD save 12 people. Aug 20th I spoke to Harvest in the Field Ministries and the LORD saved 12 more teens. THANK YOU FOR YOUR PRAYERS AND SUPPORT. Please pray for my strength because many doors have opened for me to preach the gospel of Jesus. I can't help myself, I must brag on Jesus everywhere I go. He is coming soon and I must be busy about my Father's business. Thanking you from the bottom of my heart for standing with me in winning lost souls.....

Special thanks to Sylvania Baptist and their members who were relentless in praying for the Color Wars Youth Event. A great "shout out" to D J Starling who had the vision and leadership for Color Wars and also for getting the doors open to speak to Alabama High School Football Teams. Hard Work and prayers stirred heaven and God came down and gave us great revival victory. I praise God with my whole heart!

123 NICARAGUANS ACCEPTED JESUS.
26 WERE SAVED AT PLAINVIEW.
114 DECISIONS TO ACCEPT JESUS WERE MADE AT COLOR WARS.
12 WERE SAVED AT DAVID STREET BAPTIST.

BOONE, NORTH CAROLINA

The Lord has had me on a soul-winning journey in Boone, North Carolina and at Look-Up Lodge, which is in South Carolina. While I was in Boone I went to a shopping mall where I met three young people. They allowed me to share my testimony and all three made decisions for Christ.

A daddy stood by his son as I shared my football story and the daddy got to hear his son, who also played football, accept Jesus as his savior. Later, a waitress and a cashier at Tuckers Restaurant prayed to be saved. Both said no one had ever told them the story about Jesus. Now their names are in the Lamb's Book of Life.

Look-Up Lodge hosted an incredible group of teens and their teachers. The Village School of Gaffney attended. I shared my story with them referencing Acts 9: 1-6 and the calling of Saul, who was later, named Paul. Mr. Will Bowers was there and he made a statement on Facebook about my message. He said, "GIVE IT ALL YOU GOT," and "YOU ALWAYS HAVE MORE IN THE TANK THAN YOU THINK YOU HAVE." This is exactly how we should be serving Jesus!

In the end there were eleven decisions for Jesus Christ and one young teen shared with me the calling of God on his life.

AGAPE BAPTIST CHURCH

P. O. Box 746 - 6829 Hwy 79 North
Pinson, Alabama, 35126

Rev. Herman Pair, Pastor Phone: 681-5683

August 16, 1995

Don Stanley and Dave Walton
Downtown Rescue Mission
P.O. Box 994
Spartenburg, South Carolina 29304

Dear Don and Dave,

What a joy it was to have you with us last week in **REVIVAL** with the Agape Family. You were truly used by our Lord to awake us, challenge us, and call us to repentance. There is no doubt that we know that God's prophets have been with us. Praise God for you and your absolute dedication and devotion to Him and His church.

Linda, Jeremy, and I enjoyed you staying with us. It was good for me to have you close enough to share in fellowship with you. The Lord knew that I needed to be with you during that week. You were such a wonderful encouragement to all of us.

Words cannot express my love for you two great men of God. You have had such a powerful influence on my life through your Godly walk with God. I have never known anyone who believes and walks with God like you do. You are a fresh breeze from heaven to this preacher who loves you with a brotherly love in Christ Jesus our loving Lord. My life will never be the same again because of your genuineness. Don't ever let anybody change you except our Lord.

Enclosed are copies of two of my tapes that I preached recently. "It's Time To Seek The Lord" was preached on July 2, 1995, Patriotic Service and the beginning of our Revival emphasis. The "Consecrated Commitment to Christ" was preached this past Sunday after you were here. I pray that God will use them in your lives and others should you desire to share them. In both of these sermons there was a powerful anointing of God on my life.

Keep praying for us that **REVIVAL** will continue here at Agape and will spread through Pinson, Jefferson County, Alabama, our nation, and around the world. Never have I been so hungry for God to supernaturally move among His people, my life, the Christians in Pinson, and to the lost. Even so, do it quickly, Lord!

May our Lord bless you as you continue to exalt Jesus and proclaim Him to the lost, the hurting, the homeless, the hopeless, and the backslidden. His power is on you, His Spirit indwells you, and His glory shines through you. Praise God!

Call me often and come to see me. If God wills, I will see you in September at Crestway Baptist Church, Birmingham. I am praying for a great harvest of souls!

In His Glorious Grace,
Herman
Herman Pair
John 3:30

Our Name Spells Love

April 25, 2008

Dave Walton
P.O. Box 349
Roebuck, S.C. 29376

Dear Dave,

Thank you for speaking to our students on April 25, 2008. Your willingness to share your testimony and witness of what Jesus has done in your life, is greatly appreciated.

The seed has once again been sowed, the increase is sure to follow. Again, my thanks.

Sincerely
In Christ

Dr. David C. Bult
Headmaster

"ACADEMIC EXCELLENCE IN A CHRISTIAN ENVIRONMENT"
P.O. Box 151 Dillon, SC 29536 (843) 841-1000/0810

YOU CAN MAKE A DIFFERENCE!

Bro. Dave,
The seniors in my classes were so pumped up after the assembly program yesterday. They were excited about the message you brought to them, and the fact that a large number of them took a stand against making wrong decisions! I believe this is the beginning of something huge! To God be the glory, great things He has done and is going to do in the lives of the students here at Hatton High! Keep us in your prayers!
In Christ,
Rhonda Nesmith

Not since 1906 has there been an out-pouring of GOD's power (an awaking). Have we come to a day where every man does that which is right in his own eyes? I have found that if we don't stand for something we will fall for anything !! For years we have had organized anti-abortion efforts yet 1.5 million babies murdered annually. We have Citizens for Decency yet 2.5 billion a year use dial-a-porn. Our Mothers against Drunk Drivers do an awesome job yet one-half of all fatalites are caused by alcohol. Suicide in the number one killer among our young people. And these stats continue to grow at an alarming rate. We are full of things and pleasure yet our hearts are empty. Health Communities provide free needles for addicts and condoms for safe sex. America spends millions on oil spills and clean up yet the needs of the poor and aged are ignored. Humane shelters are built for stray animals yet 3 million precious Americans live on the streets. The neglect of the poor and the needy is always an index for spiritual emptiness. We are looking for happiness and fulfillment in all the wrong places. And then there is our homosexual crisis. Need I say more. Greed has swept our land. Violence fills our citics. Gangs roam the streets We have left our children grasping at straws of hopelessness and have not given them a solid rock to stand upon. IMMORALITY like a cess-pool flows into our homes each day. (child abuse,child prostitution,incest,divorce,,jails overcrowded, porn-no, lying, stealing). We have sinned greatly and don't even blush.....our own iniquities testify against us. We look in the mirror and see that the enemy is us. If we take a real hard look we will see that the enemy is not the misguided youth, not corrupt public officials, greedy businessmen, homosexuals, drug addict, are anything else. These are only the symptoms of the disease. The real problem is the believers in the church of the LORD JESUS CHRIST. We have failed to up-hold holiness. We have sealed our lips in the streets and do not declare the name of JESUS. We have become ashamed of the name JESUS. We have become pew-fillers, lukewarm,halfhearted commitments, faint hearted,clouds without water,trees with withered fruit——prayer closet empty, prayer altars broken down, watchmen asleep, intercessors silent............We are barren,fruitless,spiritless, and we are twice plucked up by the roots. All of this bothers me but the truth can set us free if we make application to the truth and repent and cry out for ourselves and our nation.

Dear PASTOR, LET'S HAVE REVIVAL

These REEBOK Shoes are 17 years old. They have walked 1000's of miles for the cause of CHRIST. These shoes have gone to into prisons, churches, schools, ankle deep mud in Nicaragua, prisons in Nicaragua and South Africa as well as prisons in the USA. These shoes have walked in the TRASH DUMP of Nicaragua and have seen the children near starvation. These shoes travel to give hope to the hurting through the name of Jesus Christ. If these shoes could talk they would tell you of the tears shed for the souls of the lost. They could tell you of the sleepless nights and the tear stained eyes weeping over families who are in trouble with their children and marriage. These shoes have traveled into nursing homes and hospitals and have seen some accept Jesus before departing from this earth. These shoes have played soccer, basketball and baseball with orphans. Some days these shoes have walked and walked and walked until they could walk NO MORE. They had seen too much suffering, too many tears, and even death. These shoes have seen blisters and blood flowing into them as they walked a little further seeking one more soul for Jesus. These shoes have preached in Mega Churches, small churches, street corners, McDonalds, Burger King, and Conferences. These shoes are always ready to travel at the sound of the Fathers voice. If these shoes could talk they would tell you how much I LOVE YOU! How much I pray for you! God is alive in me and I desire to share HIM with everyone.

These shoes have stood in muddy creeks and rivers of Nicaragua baptizing new converts in the faith. I believe if I were to ask my shoes, where is the favorite place in all the places you have gone you would like to go back to. I believe you would hear my shoes say, the TRASH DUMPS of Nicaragua. A place where I saw trash hearts, starving children, hurting families cry out to the LIVING GOD for salvation. And GOD was faithful and came down and revealed HIMSELF and HIS powerful love for these incredible people. I pray that God keeps my shoes in good shape for another 17 years. My shoes are all about my Fathers business and I would not doubt that He would allow me to be wearing them the day He takes me home. I'm preparing now for my next mission trip into Nicaragua. PASTOR, I long for these shoes to come To your city. I desire to meet your people and share with them what great things GOD IS DOING! I Am a SBC EVANGELIST from S.C. Please pray about My coming for a ONE DAY MEETING or a FULL REVIVAL!!!

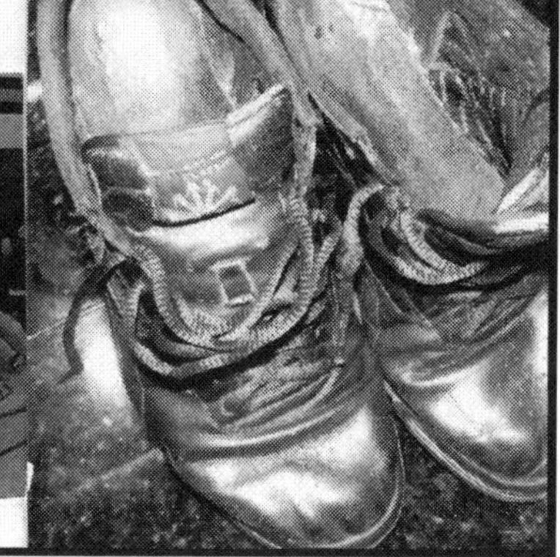

Isaiah 52: 7

SOUL WINNING JOURNEY CONTINUES

God is pouring out His Spirit on us in our revivals. In a recent revival the Pastor's son Wilson called me and said, "the Lord continues to save souls and preacher Dave the glory of the Lord is falling at First Baptist."

I have been mentoring Edgar Mendoza for 4 years in market place evangelism and prison ministry. In 3 weeks he has seen a harvest of 178 souls. He saw 130 saved at Strawberry Hill Farms and the rest in prison outreach. To God be the Glory!

I do not like giving numbers but it is the only way I can show what great things the Lord is doing. In 18 church revivals, 4 rehab centers, 2 missions, 4 TV appearances, 2 sports camps, 2 prisons, one mission trip into Nicaragua, and street ministry the Lord has given us over 300 souls for the Lord's kingdom. In one meeting several young people accepted the call to preach and to be missionaries. Glory to God!

My heart cries out for lost souls to be saved. I am praying for you my partners and your extended families that all come to the saving knowledge of Jesus Christ. Time is short and we must be serious about sharing our story with a lost and dying world. Your prayers and support are vital for us to remain on the front lines for Jesus. Thank you for your faithfulness in giving to this ministry! We remain RELENTLESS in the pursuit of lost souls. Please pray for my health, our traveling, and more open doors to preach the gospel.

All That is Important in Life is Winning ...

EVANGELIST DAVE WALTON

Lost Souls to Christ!

"Bragging on Jesus" Romans 1:16

PLEASE HELP ME FINISH STRONG IN 2013

My heart is so full. So much I desire to do for the LORD. I'm excited about finishing strong in ministry for 2013 and I'm excited about the opportunities that are before us for 2014.

REVIVAL doors are already opening for 2014. Our MISSION NICARAGUA is set for August 2-9-2014.

Our commitment to win souls each day has never changed. Our heart cry is to seek the lost at any cost. I do remember what it feels like to be lost. I remember our entire family being saved on the same day (September 7, 1975). The fire burns in me from the LORD to lift Jesus up daily as HE draws the lost to HIM.

We are committed to the feeding centers in Nicaragua where children come to church and receive a hot meal after church every week. Many are accepting Jesus as they see the hands of Jesus at work. I was hungry and you fed me!

We are entering our 4th month in providing food for the children and the elderly at Pisgah Cotton Mill Town in NC. God has given us a mighty harvest of souls in this OUTREACH.

LORD willing we hope to build another church in Nicaragua in 2014, and build several homes for poor families. We continue to support these families with discipleship programs. Thank you so much for your SUPPORT and PRAYERS.

SPEAKING ON SOUL WINNING AT THE SBC PASTORS CONFERENCE

Informing and Inspiring South Carolina Baptists

February 4, 2010

ceding each meeting, the SCBC and area associations will host GPS rallies at 6 p.m. Fagg and Ron Barker, SCBC evangelism and prayer strategist, will preach at the rallies, and host churches (Northwood and Anderson Mill Road) will provide music.

The conferences' Monday sessions will begin at 9:30 a.m. The afternoon will include GPS workshops from 2-4 p.m. Invitation-only dinners for baptism leaders from associations will be held at 4:30. Evening sessions will begin with music at 6 p.m., followed by worship and preaching.

On Tuesday morning, the sessions will begin at 10 a.m. There will be three speakers and music focused on how to reach the next generation with the gospel, Fagg said. A detailed schedule is available at *www.scbaptist.org*.

Speakers for the Northwood conference include Will Browning, Roy Fish, Sammy Galbreath, Sonny Holmes, Mark Mittelburg, Frank Page and Frank Shivers. Charleston Southern University's New Vision and Northwood Baptist Church will lead the music.

Speakers at the Anderson Mill Road conference include Jay Hardwick, D.J. Horton, Frank Page, David Platt, Alvin Reid and Dave Walton. North Greenville University's Joyful Sound and Anderson Mill Road's music ministry will lead the music.

"These are critical times for our nation and world," said Fagg. "If the church is going to be the church, we need to urgently take the whole gospel to the whole world that all might be whole. These conferences are opportunities to be motivated and equipped to accomplish this task from across the street to the ends of the earth."

AMAZING MISSION TRIP TO NICARAGUA

This trip into Nicaragua was life changing. To have the opportunity to hug and love on orphans and senior citizens at a nursing home was just GOD AWESOME! I got to see my orphan son Christopher, a delight of my heart. He quoted two Bible verses as I hugged him. At the orphanage we provided ice cream for the residents and it was a sight to see. Ice cream all around their lips and on their nose. It was a Ha Ha moment.
At the nursing home lap quilts were provided for the residents and it was a big hit. We provided sweet bread and juice for them and they were so thankful.
Revival at the Church at the Parcels was God ordained. Lives were changed as the entire church came forward wanting to be God's witness in their area. We served a hot meal of beans and rice and chicken after church to all who attended. This church is headed up by Pastor Francisco, and is on fire for Jesus. They are having people join nearly every Sunday and people being baptized on a regular bases. To GOD be all the glory!
Our team spent Wednesday preparing for a wedding. Food to prepare, and decorations for the first wedding I ever attended in Nicaragua. One of our orphan children who has grown into a God fearing man was married to Jennial and we were there to be a part. A bathroom and shower was built by this team as an add on to the wedding couple's home. Praise God for our partners who made this possible. THANK YOU>>>THANK YOU! We also praise God for the 40 souls he allowed us to see saved. The Lord was truly with us as we lifted up the name of JESUS! Thank you for your FAITHFULNESS in helping Dave Walton Ministries reach the lost and the poor of this world. Blessings to you!

LIVING THE GOD MIRACLE

In 1972, I graduated from Limestone College, and in September of 1972, I applied for work at the Regency Health Spa, in the Pinewood Shopping Center. I got the job and would later be promoted to Club Manager in 1973. The Spa consisted of weight lifting machines, arm curl machines, tread mills, and much more to help people get their bodies in shape.

I remember one year we were on a membership drive and we contacted Dennis Tinerino, an American bodybuilder who held records as a four time Mr. Universe, Mr. America, and Hall of Famer. He put on a show like no one else and we broke records on membership enrollment that day.

Dennis and I became friends and stayed in touch for quite a while. We also had Lee Haney work out at our Spa for a short time. Lee shares the all-time record for Mr. Olympia titles at eight with Ronnie Coleman. Lee Haney is my favorite Pro Bodybuilder and a legend in his own right. I really enjoyed this type of work because I was helping people get their bodies in better shape, thus producing a better lifestyle physically and emotionally. In 1975, a man came to join our Spa by the name of Mr. Dub Grant and I was to introduce him to his workout and help him get in shape. Well, I worked him out like a rented mule and then I discovered he was sixty-two-years old.

Dub was a great gentleman and in our conversation stated he knew me from my football days as QB at Spartanburg High School Crimson Tide. How is that, I asked?" He almost called the Dorman vs. Spartanburg High of 1965 play by play. I was truly amazed at his memory. He closed his remarks by stating; "I saw the 64 yard run you had in that game that beat the opposing team." He then asked me to have lunch with him and I accepted. We became friends and he would often take me out for a meal. I later discovered that he knew of my daddy's boxing career. We had long talks about football and boxing and I grew fond of Mr. Grant.

He continued coming to the Spa for a long period of time and then one day he left the Spa and I did not see him again. Some 30 days passed and one evening I received a phone call from Mr. Grant asking me to do him a favor of which I agreed. The favor I would learn was to go to church with him the coming Sunday morning and I agreed to go with him but I was in hopes I could meet him at the church he was going to so that if I decided to change my mind I could make up so off the wall excuse of not making it there. Mr. Grant said, "No way, I'm coming to pick you up and we will go together." I think Mr. Grant had a plan and was working it out! I went to church with him, September 7, 1975 at Arch Street Baptist and the rest is history. My life was changed forever because of Jesus Christ.

You would think my getting saved would be enough for Mr. Grant but that is not the case. January of 1976, I was to speak at our church on what is called, Men's Day. Mr. Grant purposed we advertise the meeting and I strongly disagreed but Mr. Grant won out, stating that "many of your friends will come to see if this is real and you will have a chance to introduce them to Jesus". I was thinking how unbelievable this seemed because I thought he was trying to make a preacher out of me, and that was not going to happen! Well the day came for me to preach my first sermon and I had studied hard and felt prepared. Pastor said you have about 30 minutes to preach your message and I thought that is just not enough time. Well, that first sermon lasted about 7 minutes. I preached all I knew about the Bible and said to myself, that's it and I am done with preaching. It is amazing how God works for it took until 1983 before I would accept the call to preach God's word. Somehow I believe Mr. Grant and my Grandmother, who are in heaven, were working out a God plan for my life, and I am forever grateful. I am truly living the God miracle!

Dennis Tinerino an American Bodybuilder.

CHAMPIONSHIP FOOTBALL TEAM

I have a tremendous heartbeat for young people. I have made it my business to try and encourage as many as I can to make the right choices. As one who speaks from experience, football players seem to pay close attention as I give them details of my failures as a MVP Quarterback. You see, I have been where they are and I warn them of the pitfalls of not paying close attention to their choices in life. Wrong decisions can cost you years of your life, as it did mine. No one has to travel that path of destruction!

While speaking to one group of football players, the Lord was with me in power and I knew something was going on beyond me. I spoke of not wanting to live because of my many failures. I told them how one man fasted and prayed over my soul. Upon finishing my talk with this championship football team, a young player pulled me aside and shared his story. He wanted to harm himself. He said, “Today I was ready to end it all but I heard your message and now I am a follower of Jesus and I feel a heavy load was taken off of my shoulders.”

Only God can do these things! His love is far reaching and He cares for all of His people. Maybe you are facing some difficult situations right now. I encourage you to do what this young athlete did that day. Call on Jesus and trust Him to take care of the problem. Go ahead and do it now!

Making Right Choices (14 Saved!)

JASON BROYLES

Here is a quick review of the last 24 hours. Just so you are aware, revival is happening right now in Dekalb County. It is starting with our kids. I believe it is time for us adults to join them. SBC has been on our knees praying expectantly for this to happen. Matthew 7 says that our Father wants to give, "good things", but we have to ask for them. We ask and the Father has given us something SO GOOD in the last 24 hours. I pray this is only the beginning!

Brother Dave Walton is definitely an anointed preacher of the Word, but you know what? He isn't gifted with some rare, unusual, special heavenly power that brings people into the saving knowledge of the Lord. Well, that's exactly what that power is! That same gift has been given to every Christian! Know the difference? He actually uses it! Thank you to these coaches who allowed Brother Dave to come in and share with their players his salvation story. The mountain is on fire with souls being saved daily.

Color Wars 2017, Sylvania Baptist Church

Twelve football players received Christ in this photo. During the Color Wars 115 players gave their hearts to Jesus. While our nation may be up in arms over issues of hatred, God is demonstrating His love toward us...while we are yet sinners. He died for you. He died for our enemies. That is the BIG deal. He loves us ALL!

EYE WITNESS TESTIMONY OF THE COLOR WARS

August 16, 2017

Words cannot express what took place tonight! We had an encounter with God. Thank you each and every one of the adults who helped and made this happen.

Also, thank you to all the churches that participated.

We saw **115 decisions for Jesus tonight**! God has moved in this area over the past several days. If you are reading this, you need to know that God loves you!

Yes, again, thanks to all and especially **Evangelist Dave Walton**.

Until Color Wars 2018!

D. J. Starling, Youth Minister

EYE WITNESS TESTIMONY OF THE COLOR WARS

August 17, 2017

God is faithful. For any of my friends who haven't heard, God showed up at SBC and on Sand Mountain, this week. Last night, we had over 280 teens and many adults participate in our second annual Color Wars. 115 of these teens stood to say they had made decisions for Christ! 115 souls. WOW!!

This is in addition to over 70 from Fyffe, Plainview, and Sylvania High Schools' football teams and FCAs. Praise the Lord!

We are thankful for Brother DAVE WALTON, who was faithful to preach God's word. Now, our job as Christians and church members is to mentor these teens and disciple them, so they will continue to grow.

Deb Sizemore

Tossing all the different dry paint into the air, they run as color descends and they are squirted with water. It is unity at its best.

East Rutherford Middle School
259 E. Church Street, P O Box 189
Bostic, NC 28018

East Rutherford Middle School
Fellowship of Christian Athletes

Mr. Dave Walton
PO Box 349
Roebuck, SC 29376

Dear Dave,

Our FCA was blessed by your testimony. Over 110 students and staff turned out to hear you speak on Monday, February 9. I was hopeful that many would come, but I was truly in awe when so many turned out. Over 35 students made a commitment to Jesus Christ that morning. Praise God for the way you have chosen to use you life. Your testimony helped these children understand that they are to be disciples in this world. Your presence here brought new commitments that will change the paths of countless others as they go and live for Jesus.

Please plan to come here every year to speak to our FCA.

Yours in Christ,

Christopher C. Parks, Sr.

Christopher C. Parks, Sr.
FCA Sponsor
8th Grade Teacher
Head Wrestling Coach

Diane Walton Tells her story in Nicaragua

I can hardly believe it is September. This year has been incredible so far in reaching the lost for Christ. Our ministry work in Nicaragua is producing much fruit and we are very grateful. You have been a part of building 7 new homes for poor families in Nicaragua and several outhouses. We were partners with another ministry in building a new church in Nicaragua in February and today the church is full of members. It was awesome to preach there this August. To God be the glory!

On another note you have been involved in training many young champions for Jesus. Currently we are training 12 young men in "Market Place Evangelism." I will speak at a Pastor's Associational Meeting this week and they have ask for me to speak on soul winning.

This year I have had the opportunity to preach in schools, prisons, churches and street corners in Nicaragua, America, and South Africa. Everywhere I go people are hurting and discouraged and I give them the answer…JESUS! Only a few days ago the Lord allowed me to share my testimony with a security guard. God was with me. He came to Jesus and said, "I wish I could have heard this earlier in life."

Across South Carolina, Alabama, North Carolina and Tennessee where I have been preaching the people are crying out for REVIVAL. Some say, "What is wrong with us?" Others say, "we need a move of God in our churches." Others have said, "I go to church and come away empty." Folks we need REVIVAL!!!!! We must turn to God with our whole hearts. We must PRAY…PRAY…PRAY. Thanks again for helping us reach the lost.

Acts 1:8 But ye shall receive power, after that the Holy Ghost is come upon you: and ye shall be witnesses unto me both in Jerusalem, and in all Judaea, and in Samaria, and unto the uttermost part of the earth.

Diane Walton tells of her experiences in Nicaragua.

We have just finished " Every Believer A Witness" at Sylvania Baptist Church. It was an exciting time as believers caught fire on telling their story. Each night members would tell how they ministered in the market place each day. They told stories of how they passed out gospel tracts and how the LORD led them to certain people to tell their testimonies to. One story that stands out is when Dale Starling went to help with "Release Time" at a nearby school. Some 65 young people had gathered together for this special time for bible study. Dale says " I was moved to read my story to these young people that I had written while in the revival of "Every Believer A Witness." To my amazement after reading my story, several youth ask me questions about being saved. After all was said and done 8 young people received Christ. (May we just keep bragging on JESUS just like Dale Starling)

Keith Atchley a teacher at Sylvania High School invited me to speak to the FCA Chapter Tuesday morning of the revival. I really look forward to speaking to the youth of America on making RIGHT decisions. These are urgent times we live in !! The enemy has attacked our youth with a vengeance. It is urgent that we take ACTION. I shared with the youth of Sylvania the bad choices I had made as a teenager, and the shame I put on my mom and dad. I also shared how I came to JESUS and ask the students if they would like to ask Christ into their lives. Several students unashamed prayed to be saved. We give all the praise to the LORD. Schools need more teachers like Keith Atchley. Please continue to remember me in your prayers. Thank you.....Dave

"That at the name of Jesus every knee should bow" Philippians 2:10

PIEDMONT WILDERNESS INSTITUTE
20238 Hwy 72 East, Clinton, SC 29325
Phone: (864) 833-4505 Fax: (775) 314-9192

January 6, 2009

Dave Walton Ministries
P.O. Box 349
Roebuck, SC 29376

Dear Walton,

We sincerely appreciate your willingness to speak to our students on December 20, 2008. Your ministry was a blessing to our youth.

Piedmont Wilderness Institute (PWI) is a non-profit program designed to help at-risk youth between the ages of 14-17 years. PWI works in partnership with the Department of Juvenile Justice. We appreciate local support such as yours as it demonstrates to our students that others do care.

Again, thank you for taking a part in our work with the youth of South Carolina.

Sincerely,

Rickie Hardy,
Executive Director

TOGETHER WE ARE PLUNDERING HELL TO POPULATE HEAVEN!

The urgency of the mission we are on grips me relentlessly and compels me to continue on in this work we do together. WE ARE IN A BATTLE FOR SOULS! Our enemy, satan tries to lull the church into indifference towards the millions of people who need salvation. There's the temptation to think that it is someone else's job or calling…or that it will happen regardless of what we do.

189 SAVED IN 4 DAY CRUSADE

Evangelist Dave Walton

PO Box 349 • Roebuck, SC 29376 • 864.573.4356

189 SAVED IN 4 DAY CRUSADE

Henagar youth revival features two with extraordinary stories: DON STANLEY DAVE WALTON

Henagar Baptist Church
Henagar, Alabama

Pastor Robert Jones

"It's SuperNAtural"

Henagar members had been praying and believing God for a supernatural move of the Lord in the 1988 REVIVAL. Night after night the Lord met with us, and the altars were filled with young people repenting and crying out to God for a changed life. Several members stated, "we were ripe for revival." Prayer meetings were the difference maker one young teenage stated. True joy filled the church and many lives were changed forever.

Luke 19:10 For the Son of man is come to seek and to save that which is lost

"That at the name of Jesus every knee should bow" Philippians 2:10

PO Box 1000
Ellenboro NC 28040
Phone: (828) 453-0186
FAX: (828) 453-0750
Email: libertybapt60399@bellsouth.net

LIBERTY BAPTIST CHURCH

Pastor: Owen Duncan ♦ Associate Pastor: Alan Beane ♦ Youth Pastor: Howard Lederfind, Jr. ♦ Music: Donald Owens

I've never known anyone more zealous to win souls to Christ than Evangelist Dave Walton. He reminds me of a biblical prophet with his anointed ability to stir the people of God out of complacency to new levels of complete surrender to the Lord Jesus Christ. I commend him to any pastor seeking someone who is bold enough to confront their church with God's truth and challenge them to live accordingly.

Brother Dave was recently with us for a crusade and the results were amazing. In three area schools we saw dozens of young people give their lives to Christ. I commend him without any reservation whatsoever.

Owen Duncan, Pastor
Rev.12:11

"...and I will walk at liberty for I seek your precepts."
Psalm 119:45

CHASE HIGH FOOTBALL

I called Dr. Fred Wolfe just moments before I was to speak to the Chase High School Football Team. His praying for me put a great passion for souls into me to see these young football players come to JESUS!

A young high school student named Ashley had organized this event. She had Liberty Baptist to furnish steaks, potatoes, green beans, and salad to the players for this first time ever event. All 36 players came to eat.

After eating we all went upstairs to the youth room, inside the church. The Lord Jesus came into the meeting. His glory was all around. I spoke to them about wrong decisions I had made in my life. How I had lost all of my sports scholarships due to an alcohol problem. Then I shared the greatest decision I ever made in my life. I asked Jesus to forgive me of my sins and come into my heart. He saved my soul. The salvation net was cast and 18 football players received JESUS!

WOW. Praise the Lord. All glory to Him. He is worthy!

CONVICTION FILLED THE ROOM

In Sylacauga, Alabama 35 rough, tough, rawhide football players bowed their knees to Jesus. Then a door opened to speak to a full assembly of students and 36 students prayed, asking Jesus into their hearts.

In Gilbertown, Alabama 38 football players were saved. In one small class room setting we saw 7 saved.

In Startex, South Carolina 10 souls were saved. Many left the church telling others of their story of salvation. From there I went to Chapman High to speak at the FCA. 70 students prayed with me.

Visiting a nursing home in the area I saw a childhood friend. He turned his life over to Jesus during that visit. While we were rejoicing I received a call to visit Spartanburg Regional Heart Center. I found a lifelong friend there in need and we prayed together, as he received Jesus.

From youth rallies to the street corners, we are seeing people saved and we give all the glory to our Lord Jesus Christ.

Revelation 3: 8 I know they works:
behold I have set before thee an open door,
and no man can shut it.

Coffeeville High School

P.O. Box 130
Coffeeville, Alabama 36524

Joe W. Shanks
Principal

(251) 276-3227

November 3, 2004

Dear Reverend Walton,

It was our pleasure to have you speak to the students at Coffeeville High School today. Our school is off the "beaten path" and someone who cares enough to make the time to speak with our 7-12 students about the dangers of making the wrong choices is greatly appreciated. Our students enjoyed your presentation. Several have been by the office since you left to see if you could come back next week. You have a tremendous gift that allows you to speak and motivate students to choose life over the death of alcohol and drugs. The number of students who raised their hands to commit to not using alcohol and drugs was very impressive.

Also, the young man that you spoke with after your presentation comes from a broken home where his parents are mostly absent from his life. Right now, Michael is at a point in his life where his choices will affect his future dramatically. He is a star on the football field, basketball court and in the classroom. Positive role models are so necessary for him and hearing the message of your struggles as a young man really inspired him.

Thank you again and please return to our campus whenever you are in this area.

Sincerely,

Joe W. Shanks

Joe W. Shanks, Principal

ljd

Straightway Ministries
...straightway they left their nets and followed him.

Pastor: Kevin Garris
310 S. Nichols St. Nichols, SC 29581

Dear Brother Dave,

Our spring revival was on for the record books as far as I am concerned. I was amazed to see so many teenagers come under Holy Ghost conviction and come forward to receive Jesus as Lord and master of their lives. I know that it really shook up the old devil when he saw the tears and passion in the eyes of those young people. We as a church are going to continue to fan the fires of revival and to press forward in the good fight of faith.

As you know our revival started with a twenty- one day Daniel fast. Boy does fasting and praying work, as we saw doors open that have been shut for sometime. When we fix our eyes on Christ, He will go far and beyond what we can imagine or comprehend. School's opening their doors to the gospel of Jesus Christ, not only the private school but also a public school. I was floored immediately when I saw teenagers drop their food during lunch to listen to an evangelist. These young people so hungry for truth in their lives that they went to the head master and gained permission for a full high school assembly. A simple FCA meeting at Pee Dee Academy turning into a move of the Holy Ghost. The result was eight kids saved in the FCA meeting and a crowd to big to count responding in the full assembly. Then God allowing us access into Green-Sea Floyds high school where only three or four had been showing up to the FCA meetings and that turning into forty and twelve more receiving Christ as Savior. As the week drew to a close we had seen forty- eight first time professions not counting the full assembly at PDA.

God bless you Bro. Dave for your excitement and passion for lost souls. I pray that you continue to witness and preach both in the churches and the streets. I thank you for the challenges you set before our church family to be all that we can be for God. I thank you also for challenging us to be better witnesses for Christ, with the way you have surrendered all to go and BRAG ON JESUS!!!

May God bless you in all you do,

Bro. Kevin

Wednesday Night 7:00pm
Sunday School 10:00am
Sunday Worship 11:00am
Sunday Night 6:00pm
Cel# 843-421-1204
Home# 843-759-0243

ROOFTOP EXPERIENCE

I arrived at the church for the Soul Winning Harvest meeting and saw two roofers working on the house across the street from the church. I was compelled by the Spirit to go and testify about Jesus, the cross and His salvation. Those men listened and said YES to JESUS. I went away praising God!

I went into the church for a tailgating party for the local football team. They occupied the first three rows of the church pews. I shared Romans 1: 16, Romans 3:23, 6:23, and 10:9-10. I could hardly believe my eyes as many came forward and received Jesus. The church roared with AMENS, clapping and praises. We all gave glory to God as He invaded the church that day.

Next stop was Jonesville, South Carolina. Clients were coming for much needed groceries at the Potters Storehouse for Thanksgiving. Over 500 turkeys were distributed to needy families and many people received Jesus. I tell you that we had revival at this feeding center! We remain on the front lines for Jesus seeking lost souls. We are in the planning stages of holding two large Christmas parties for the children in Brevard and Jonesville feeding centers. It will be God awesome!

October 14th I'll host the Christian TV program of NITELINE out of Greenville South Carolina. In the meantime I am working in Chesnee with Dr. Goodroe, Rev. Daniel Godfrey, Rev. Brandon Lewis, and Pastor Ron as we plan 16 churches' simultaneous revivals in the Chesnee area.

PRAYER IS A KEY

Mark 11: 24 Whatsoever things you desire, <u>when you pray</u>, believe that you receive them, and you shall have them.

FISHERS OF MEN

Matthew 4:19 "Come, follow me," Jesus said, "and I will make you fishers of men."

And as I write witnessing moments, please remember it is not my intelligence or craftiness that sways with me and to follow the Lord, but of His presence and the drawing of the Holy Spirit. I have found an important promise I dubbed the Bible, and that is, if you will "follow Jesus" He will make you a "fisher of men."

Sometimes it is hard to explain, but a supernatural burden comes on me for a person's soul and it brings deep weeping and agonizing prayer in the secret place. **I have learned that prayer is the key to soul winning!** I began praying for Jason and the Lord spoke to my heart about taking him out to lunch in hopes of sharing my testimony with him. **I believed he would pray to receive Christ.**

I was nervous as we sat down to have a meal together. Our talk was small talk to begin with and I shared with him upfront that I was praying for him. It was amazing as I watched his eyes water and it was evidence that the Spirit was working on him.

Our lunch at Cracker Barrel was going well and soon I realized it worth the invitation for it was only moments after hearing my testimony that Jason desired to be a follower of Jesus. He bowed his head in the restaurant and prayed to be saved. It was truly a God Moment!

If you desire to be a fisher of men then cry out to the Lord in prayer and He will surly make you one!

PRAY BELIEVING

John 14:14 If you ask any thing in my name, I will do it.

I often trace back in time and events in my life that were turning points. As you get older they are easier to understand. One evening, as I was entering our home on Arch Street, I saw Grandma Sis was on her knees praying.

Trying not to make noise I walked very quietly across the floor and went to the kitchen, where Mom had supper waiting for me. Mom knew I would be coming in late because of football practice and she knew I would be starving. After I finished eating, I walked into the living room and there was Grandma still on her knees praying.

My bed was inside of a walk-in closet, just of the living room. I was ready for bed. I fell fast asleep only to be awakened by a voice sometime later. I got up and took a look from the door of the closet and there was Grandma, still praying, so I began to listen to her words. She was talking like a person was in the room with her, listening. I opened the door a bit more so I could see and hear better. (Of course, I looked first for a visitor.)

She was calling out the family's names in prayer. I remember that she called each person by their full name; and finally she got to my name. She asked God to save David O'Dell Walton and then she paused and said, "God, call him to preach."

I closed that door to my walk-in closet and I said, "God don't listen to a word she said. I am going to be a pro-ball player." **As time would tell the story, it was her prayer that got through to Heaven**. I was in a supernatural moment and did not know it until years later. Grandma passed away never knowing that I came to Jesus and that I accepted the call to preach. Or, maybe she does know!

WALLACE AND KIM NIX
CHOSEN CHILDREN MINISTRIES

I SHALL NOT DIE

**Psalm 118: 17 I shall not die, but live,
to declare the works of the Lord.**

I was getting ready to do work at our office, which was located in our home, and to be honest I was under a lot of stress. Most of it, I had put on myself. Suddenly I felt pain across my chest like needles sticking me in my arms. I fell backward to the floor and could hardly breathe. My chest like an elephant was standing on it. The noise I made brought my wife running upstairs to find out what all the commotion was about. She found me on the floor in much pain. She ran to get an aspirin and put it under my tongue. Her quick thinking saved my life!

I told her I was alright but she demanded a call to 911 and the ambulance came to take me away. It was discovered that I had a blockage in an artery and it would require a stint to relieve the problem. After the stint was put in the artery, it was amazing as I could feel the difference in breathing and I felt one hundred percent better.

Doctors decided that I needed 90 days of cardiac rehabilitation under a medically supervised program, just to be on the safe side. For almost 90 days, I exercised and got in great shape at the rehabilitation center. A week before graduation, I had another heart attack, while on the treadmill. I was rushed to a room in the center so the nurse could determine exactly what had happened.

They discovered I had another heart attack and this one had a scary name, it is called the "Widow Maker". The nurses got me stabilized as my wife, Diane, watched. I made the mistake of saying, "I'm good now, and I have a golf match at 5pm, so I need to get to the golf course." That did not sit well with Diane or the nurses; the doctor didn't like my plan.

On Monday I reported to the hospital and talked with my doctor and it was decided I would have to have bypass heart surgery. The doctor explained to me what this "Widow Maker" heart problem was and it did not sound good. He said, "Dave, if ten men had the same heart attack that you did, nine of them would have died. Dave, you have got to live. Do you believe in the sovereignty of God?" I answered him with a nod and "yes". The doctor told me to get busy and finish what God had called me to do.

The surgery was successful and I did continue to do the Lord's work. However in 2010 I had another small heart attack while watching my grandson, Walton Wyatt, play in a golf tournament.

I was walking the cart path to the next tee off when it happened. Another heart attack! I was all alone, as everyone had left to go to the 17th tee off. I cried out to God and asked for His help. The pain was severe as I fell to my knees and grabbed my chest. I looked for someone to help me, but

I was all alone. I managed to get up and walk up the hill for about 20 yards and down I fell, again. The pain in my chest was increasing. I can barely remember what happened next. I do remember getting to the 17th tee off and someone let me ride to see hole 17 and 18 played out.

At that moment I was living a miracle, for only God could have gotten me up that steep hill. Walton placed high enough to win a trophy and I would not miss that for the world. I told no one what had happened to me and we headed home. I told Walton Wyatt how proud I was of him for winning his trophy.

On Monday, I was getting ready for work when the pain stuck again. I bent over and there stood my wife, Diane. It is amazing how she turns up at the moment I need her! I was in great danger. Diane said with a loud voice, "Get in the car! I'm taking you to the emergency room." Like a good husband, I obeyed!

In route to the hospital she explained to me what to do:

"Go into the hospital.

"Go to the front desk.

"Tell them you are having a heart attack.

"Dave, they will then take you immediately back for observation."

I did what she said and they took me back to begin running tests. They discovered another blockage was the probable cause of my pain. I was scheduled for a cardio catheterization (a procedure used to diagnose and treat the condition in the artery when there is a blockage).

Another stint was put in the artery and I was back in the saddle bragging on Jesus, and searching for lost souls. I know that I am called to press toward the mark of the prize of the high calling from Jesus. I am a walking miracle and give all the glory to the Lord!

At 70 years old, the Lord has me busy building churches in Nicaragua with Wallace Nix and *Chosen Children Ministries* and going to prisons preaching the gospel with Jon Simone of *Promise Land Prison Ministry*. We feed the hungry with Rev. Terry Whitesides with Crossroads Baptist in Brevard North Carolina, and with Rev. Barney Blackwell of the Potters Storehouse in Jonesville South Carolina.

We continue to conduct revivals in churches, schools, and speak to football teams.

We deeply covet your prayers.

MY PRAYER PARTNER
DR. JOHN WILTON

Psalm 37: 23 The steps of a good man are ordered by the Lord: and he delighteth in his way"

Never did a verse mean so much to me as when I met Rev. John Wilton. Psalm 37: 23. It was a beautiful day with hardly a cloud in the sky and my grandson Walton and his sister Mary Conway were shooting basketball hoops in their backyard. There is nothing like a has-been trying to impress his grandkids, I had to complain about my bad back! You get the picture?

While playing basketball, I noticed a man on the hill watching, so I walked to where he stood and introduced myself. His name was Dr. John Wilton. I loved to listen to him talk because he is from South Africa. I shared with Mr. John that I was in South Africa in 2010, preaching in the city of Worcester. I was there for the celebration of the 150th Anniversary of the Great Awakening of South Africa with my friend and brother Edgar Mendoza. Edgar and I preached in the prison, nursing homes, churches, and the streets of Fish Hoek; which is a part of the City of Cape Town.

After some small talk, Mr. John said, "Let's pray together." We sat down on the hill and Mr. John began praying and God came down and met with us. It was a God moment for me! He poured his heart out in prayer for me to see more souls saved and for the Lord to watch over me and our family.

Each time I met with Mr. John he would quote Bible verses to me and ask me what I thought about the verse. It was amazing listening to him rightly divide the Word of God. For several years we met for prayer and for special lunch times. We always talked about Jesus. Mr. John preached all across America and I would say, I am heading to Mobile, Alabama, and he would call out several church names where he had held revivals. He was a delightful man of God to be around.

Mr. John became sick and was admitted to Spartanburg Regional Hospital. I visited him. I will never forget the visit as long as I live. He and I talked about Jesus and he asked me how revivals were going. I shared several revival God moments and then I asked if I could pray. He agreed so I knelt beside the hospital bed and prayed for Mr. John, wanting so badly for him to recover. We talked a little longer and I said it was time for me to go, because tomorrow for a revival. I held his hand and then I kissed him on his head. I told Mr. John how much I loved him. He reached for my hand and kissed it. I fought back the tears. As I was leaving the room, I began weeping as I walked down the hall. Off I went to conduct another revival, not knowing it would be the last time I would see Mr. John on earth. Yet, I rejoice that I will see him again in the resurrection.

Words fail me at this point of writing. Mr. John taught me to pray through his powerful prayers. I am forever indebted to Dr. John Wilton.

HOLLYANNE SHOPS AND BRAGS

BILO

It amazes me sometimes at the boldness of my 9 year old granddaughter, Hollyanne. We were in Bilo grocery store and I was in a hurry to get some items and head home to cook supper. Yep, supper! Momma always taught me that supper is the evening meal and she proved it in the Bible. Momma knows best! Amen?

Unbeknownst to me Hollyanne was watching two men standing about six feet and six inches tall, each, and she says to me, "Poppi, they need Jesus! Go tell them about Jesus." I was stunned and afraid to do this because I need a little time preparing myself. Now folks, this is cold turkey witnessing and I started praying! I mean really praying.

I pushed the grocery store cart near them and asked, "Hey, I bet ya'll play basketball for some college. I know both of you can dunk a basketball." They said, yes, you are right on both accounts. I asked them if I might share my story of playing football, basketball, and baseball. Surprised, they exclaimed, "You played all three sports?" I answered them that I did, and then I shared my football story as a quarterback of the Spartanburg High School Crimson Tide. I shared my climb to the top in the sports world and my decline to the pit as failure and how I brought shame and disgrace to my parents and my team.

Next, I shared how a man prayed and fasted for my soul and invited me to church. I could tell that the Holy Spirit was working on them as their eyes watered up and they listened with intentional attention to every word spoken. I could hardly believe what was happening as I cast the net for salvation. Both of these young men wanted to pray for Jesus to save their souls. WOW!

This little child led me to share Jesus when my mind was somewhere else. Thank you Hollyanne, for your alertness to the Holy Spirit's voice for these two lost souls. Their names are in the Book of Life and in the Book of Remembrance.

One day, in Heaven, Hollyanne will read their names and read about that event and those men in Bilo.

Burger King

Hollyanne and I went to Burger King where my hunger desire got lost in the smell of a char-broiled burger, hot fries and diet coke. While I was wondering if the diet coke helped my calorie count, Hollyanne was shopping for souls. We were handed our tray of food and sat down to eat. I took one bite of the Whopper and Hollyanne said, “Poppi, that cashier looks sad. I think you need to go and tell her about Jesus.”

I kept enjoying the burger, but Hollyanne refused to stop talking about the cashier. I looked around and no one was at the counter, so I went to the cashier and struck up a conversation. I then shared Jesus with her.

WOW! The young lady told me she needed Jesus! Hollyanne and I stood there praying and the young lady prayed with us to receive Jesus at the Burger King. Then out of nowhere, Hollyanne started testifying about her salvation and her love for Jesus. I tell you, it was a God moment for this grandfather to see and to hear Hollyanne bragging on Jesus.

Hollyanne praying with Poppi at the 2017 school event,
***See You at the Pole*.**

GOD IS ON TIME

KIMBERLY'S FACEBOOK MESSAGE

Hi Brother Dave!

I can't believe I finally found you on Facebook and have the opportunity to thank you, Beck, and Don for planting a seed in my life 23 years ago. And, boy, did it ever grow into something beautiful! I was so desperate to find a mother and father's love. I grew up feeling alone in life; celebrating things that I only wished my parents could celebrate with me…it just never happened. My mother never bonded with me after her divorce from my father, and it took me growing up to face that heart-wrenching truth.

While I endured much heartache during my journey, I never turned to drugs or alcohol. I am so proud of the strength and morals I held so dear. But, as preacher's daughter, I did not REALLY know God. And the absence of my father, left me struggling to understand what that kind of relationship was like.

Then I met you guys!

I had a mother figure and two father figures who would guide me to know God and set an example for me to follow. Fast forwarding to today…my testimony is very deep! I have ten kids! You remember Cheyenne as she was the first child to enter the doors of the mission? I then had Savannah who is now 18. I adopted TJ, my son, who is now 25. I then took joint custody of 3 children whose mom was murdered by their dad. Two of those children have Fragile X Syndrome. Then I took in a baby at 9 days old (she is now almost 7) who has Down syndrome. And finally, I took in 3 siblings, 5 years ago (the brothers have autism). The baby was only 13 weeks when I got him and withdrawing from drugs.

I found my true purpose and how to really…I mean REALLY…have a relationship with God by seeing world through their eyes. I never in a million years would have guessed my life would lead me in this direction. I am a huge advocate in the special needs world. I home school, work, and do some photography on the side. My schedule is busy as I have 35 specialists between all my children. But, the love and joy we share is incredible!

I never forgot where I came from. Or, the people who touched my life and left the biggest footprints! And, I can't thank you enough for planting such a huge seed in my life! God sent all the right people at the right time to water it!

Love,
Kimberly

HOSPTIAL MIRACLE

Acts 9: 40...But Peter put them all forth, and kneeled down, and prayed; and turning him to the body with Tabitha, arise, and she opened her eyes; and when she saw Peter, she sat up.

"Prayer is a shield to the soul, a sacrifice to God, and a scourge for Satan."
John Bunyan

"Prayer is an effort of will."
Oswald Chambers

I certainly do not have all the answers about prayer. Tonya called in a panic concerning her husband, David Smith. He had a heart attack, and was being admitted into the hospital. I began to pray.

I headed to the hospital as fast as I could, praying all the way. The love for my friend, knowing he was in physical trouble, brought tears to my eyes and passion to my heart to pray, pray and pray some more. David was in surgery and things did not look good. The waiting room was filled with people hoping that all was well and that David would pull through the heart attack.

We could sense all the time that God was with us and our hearts were strengthened because of His nearness. This is important. When we found out that David was out of surgery and was given a room, we rejoiced and gave God thanks. Sometime later I was allowed to go to David's hospital room. As I arrived I saw a nurse at his side. He had tubes going in every direction into his body and I could tell his heart attack had been a bad one. After all, I have had 3 heart attacks myself.

I said to the nurse, "I have come to pray for my friend and I am not sure you will want to stay." She said, "You pray and I am staying at his side to check vitals." God came into the hospital room as I began to quote Bible verses and speak life into David. A prayer hedge was placed around him. I pleaded with God to bind Satan from the room and to allow the Holy Spirit to cover David with grace, mercy, and healing.

Please know that I am a novice at this, but David is a dear friend and I prayed with great passion and with what belief I could muster up. It is hard to believe, but 45 minutes passed before I stopped praying, because I felt a release to leave.

Out in the waiting room, friends and loved ones were waiting and hoping to hear "good news". I said, "It is in God's hands and we must continue praying for David". I don't know how, but God touched my dear friend, David Smith, and he was released from the hospital several days later.

It was a miracle!

Readers, we don't have the answers! We are just called to pray. All stories don't turn out like this, but for me, I am ready to go and be with Jesus when He's ready to receive me. Let us all just agree to pray, and pray, and pray!

As I have talked to David about this season in his life, he said, "I remember hearing you, Dave, praying for me, as I would come in and out room the medication. I was aware I was in the hospital bed. My nurse told me that preacher came to my room and prayed up a storm over me and I told her it was my friend Dave Walton. She said that all she knows is that Heaven came down! I heard some of that prayer. "Don't give up! Fight to live, David! Your family needs you!"

I also asked David how did the heart attack, which put him at death's door, change his life. He replied, "I have a tremendous love for life and it brought me closer to Jesus and to my family. The desire to live was strong in my heart as I was in that hospital room, and I was so thankful for all the people who prayed for me. The strong fighting desire to live was in me. I believed I was receiving a miracle. The love for my family was a fighting force in me and I believe it brought me through the heart attack and surgery. Thank you to everyone who prayed for me!"

"One last thought," David said, "The nurse said they needed to start feeding me and I said why not call my wife Tonya back here to feed me? The nurse agreed and Tonya came to the hospital bedside and helped feed me. Around the second day Tonya said, "David I believe you can feed yourself." I told her if I could feed myself she couldn't come back in here and I wanted her here with me."

Love will win every time!

Thank you Lord for the miracle in touching David Smith's life!

HE WAS A MAN OF WAR

I am a Type 2 Diabetic and while on errands for the ministry I felt a sharp drop in my sugar. I knew I needed to get food, fast! A Hardees restaurant was near, so I headed there to get some food and overcome the horrible way I was feeling. Upon entering the restaurant I noticed there no customers. I continued to the counter to place my order. The cashier was a young man and he appeared to be in great physical shape. I ordered my food and he told me he would bring the order out to me. As I was waiting on the food, I noticed that there still no customers and that the drive-thru bell had not rang. This is very unusual for Hardees. I spoke to the Lord about this and I heard the Lord say, in my heart, "I have closed this store down for you to testify to this young man."

Moments later the young man brought my order to my table and I struck up small talk with him. I found out he had only been working for Hardees for three months. He stated he was in the war in Afghanistan for one year and when he arrived home that Hardees hired him. I shook his hand and I thanked him or fighting for our freedom!

I said to him, "No customers and no drive-thru action. You are a man of war. Do you recognize what is going on here at this moment?"

He replied, "I don't, sir, but I got a feeling you are going to answer this for me."

"Young man," I replied, "God has shut this store down so that I can testify of the greatness of my God and His great love for you." After giving my short version of my salvation story he said, "Your story is a lot like mine. I have alcohol problems, bitterness, unforgiveness, and a lot more problems but I need what you got!" I said, "Let's pray." But, he said, "We are not in a church." I said, "God said it is okay to pray."

We did pray and Robert came to trust in Jesus Christ for his salvation. Upon finishing praying, customers started coming into the restaurant and the drive-thru bell started ringing.

For two years I visited Robert, taking study material to help him grow spiritually. I know this was a divine appointment that only God could bring about, and I believe Robert's friends, mom, and grandmother had been praying for him to have an encounter with Jesus. God will use what he desires and this time it was my sugar drop from diabetes.

To God be the glory!

MAKING RIGHT CHOICES

I have been given the opportunity to speak in many schools and the one thing that registers in one's mind is that you hope you are making a difference. It is always a joy to receive a letter from a coach telling you that the students considered the meeting a life-changing experience.

This letter arrived from the FCA meeting at East Rutherford Middle School in Bostic, North Carolina. I spoke on "Making Right Choices". Some 110 students attended. The letter is from Coach Christopher C. Parks, Sr.

East Rutherford Middle School
259 E. Church Street, P O Box 189
Bostic, NC 28018

East Rutherford Middle School
Fellowship of Christian Athletes

Mr. Dave Walton
PO Box 349
Roebuck, SC 29376

Dear Dave,

Our FCA was blessed by your testimony. Over 110 students and staff turned out to hear you speak on Monday, February 9. I was hopeful that many would come, but I was truly in awe when so many turned out. Over 35 students made a commitment to Jesus Christ that morning. Praise God for the way you have chosen to use you life. Your testimony helped these children understand that they are to be disciples in this world. Your presence here brought new commitments that will change the paths of countless others as they go and live for Jesus.

Please plan to come here every year to speak to our FCA.

Yours in Christ,

Christopher C. Parks, Sr.

Christopher C. Parks, Sr.
FCA Sponsor
8th Grade Teacher
Head Wrestling Coach

GOD GOT THE LAST WORD

I have been in a lot of church revivals since 1983 and many stand out, but this one is for the records!

She came night after night to the revival and I believe she wore the same dress. There was a shine about her and smile that was eye catching. The revival was scheduled for Sunday through Wednesday night...unless something happened...a God moment...and then we would have to extend the meeting.

Night after night the Lord showed up and many lives were changed from the preaching of the Word. On the final night it happened! I don't think anyone was prepared for what we would hear from this middle school girl.

She said, "We can't stop this revival. I went to the principal today and asked if the evangelist could come and speak to our middle school students."

That was a shocker!

She continued telling us her story and we were amazed as she described going to the principal and making this request. She said, the principal said no, because there was no room for this event as the calendar was filled with many events that month.

She said, "I went to the little girls room and made the john my prayer altar. I cried out to God to change the principal's mind because drugs and alcohol are in our school and students need help." She stated, "I made my way back to the principal's office because I felt the Lord leading me. When I arrived at the door of his office it was as if I had a free path. I took it. I asked the principal to reconsider his stance on the evangelist coming to speak to our students. I don't know what happened that day, but God got the last word with my principal. He said 'YES, he can come and speak.' He set the time, so, we must go!"

Revival in Sylacauga, Alabama

by

Pastor Max Buttram
First Baptist Church of Oak Grove

We had an amazing 4-day revival at First Baptist Church of Oak Grove in Sylacauga, Alabama in April 2017. Brother Dave Walton was our evangelist and he came on fire for souls!

A few days before the revival started, I made a visit to see the head football coach at Sylacauga, High School. I wanted to ask if he would allow Bro. Dave to speak to his football team. He said he would try to bring a busload to the revival one night. (I wasn't too hopeful that he would keep that commitment.)

After Bro. Dave arrived in town for revival, the Lord led us to pay a visit to the football coach on Monday afternoon. After meeting Bro. Dave in person the coach invited him to speak to his 9th grade football team the following day. But that didn't happen! An hour before our appointment the coach called to cancel the meeting because of a conflict in schedule. But God didn't shut the door! The coach said, "if you can come tomorrow I'll have the team ready." That was Wednesday, the last day of our revival. It proved to be perfect in God's timing!

When we arrived the 9th grade football team was working out in the weight room. The coach instructed them to go into the locker room, sit on the floor, and give Bro. Dave their attention. Bro Dave shared with them his football testimony and how Jesus had transformed his life. He asked them to repeat a prayer of commitment to Jesus, and then asked all who prayed that prayer to stand. All 23 players stood in response! Then they gathered in a huddle, raised their hands together, and said 1-2-3 Praise Jesus! What a powerful God-moment.

Later the same day we had a pizza blast at the church for the young people prior to the closing night of revival. Bro. Dave shared his testimony, gave an invitation, and 35 young people said "yes" to Jesus! What an incredible day it was in Sylacauga, Alabama.

God is continuing to work in our city as many in our congregation are now "bragging on Jesus." Our church pianist, who owns a business in town, had the opportunity to lead a former employee to Jesus when he stopped in for a visit the week following revival.

God had done great things in Sylacauga and will continue as we are faithful to tell our story of what Jesus has done for us.

BE FAITHFUL TO YOUR CALLING

The calling to preach revivals in churches will take you into the unknown. I have conducted revivals in churches with 12 members, 18 members, 300 members, and with several thousand members.

You will learn, as you travel for the Lord, to be flexible as He conducts revivals, that He reserves the right to add things to the revival. He may send you to speak, then open another door in that same location to speak to a high school, or somewhere else.

Such was the case with Pastor Brad in Gilbertown Alabama. The church had about 100 members coming to the revival each night. I was excited about preaching and hoping someone would receive Jesus as Lord. To be honest, not much was happening... probably my preaching. A radio station opened the door for me to testify live on their station and by all means I did!

It was great because it was done outside on a porch and people would come by and honk their car horn at us. Now, that is Alabama!

Then it happened!

The preacher's son played football and he had a conversation with his coach about my playing football in high school. He asked the coach if I could come and speak to the team after practice. The coach agreed and a date and time was set.

I arrived early to watch their practice session and really was impressed with the team. After the practice ended, the coach and players led me to the football theater room where they watch films of the next week's football opponents. As best as I can remember there were about 60 players in this room. I was thankful for this opportunity to speak to this championship football team.

The coach introduced and left the room. My heart was pounding but I knew God was with me and I knew He was the One who opened this door for me to speak. Having prayed through the night, I heard the Lord say to me to speak about my failures and wrong decisions, then, I was to share how I came to know the Living God. God put words in my mouth to say and they were hitting the mark.

I spoke to them about total commitment to Jesus. I shared how to be an overcomer, and how to live the surrendered life for Christ.

It was time to cast the net for salvation! It was amazing as 47 football players stood up to pray and to repent of sins and ask Jesus into their heart. I was overwhelmed at the number of players responding to the altar call. We prayed out loud to receive Jesus and it was incredible music to my ears.

Some of these rough – n – tough football players began to weep and I knew God was doing a mighty work in them. Many players came to me and thanked me for coming. They made a request. As a team they said, "Preacher, will you go and talk with our coach about being saved? We will go with you and stand outside the door and pray."

I agreed and went to the coach's office. Several coaches were in the room with him. I zeroed in on the head coach and shared wit him about my battle with alcohol and how a man prayed and fasted over my soul. Only God could have set this up, because he was ready for a change in his life. When I shared that his football team was outside his office door praying for him, it broke the hold of the enemy over him and prayed to be saved!

Glory to God! It was the Lord's doing! I have learned to GO TELL no matter what it looks like. Go tell people about Jesus and watch Jesus go to work in drawing people into the Kingdom of God.

I have given it my best, even at the age of 70 years old. I am still preaching in schools, prisons, churches, to football teams, and anywhere the Lord will open a door. Be faithful to your calling as an evangelist.

PASTOR RONNIE HELMS

I remember this meeting well, in First Baptist Indian Trail. As the students began to come into the church auditorium I started weeping. I excused myself and went to the men's restroom where I locked myself in a stall and began to cry and weep for their souls. I said to the Lord, "I am incapable o speaking to these young people. Lord, please help me say the right words so many will come to know You as their savior."

As I made my way back to the auditorium I could hardly believe the amount of young people attending this school. I was introduced to the students as the speaker and as I approached the podium to bring the message, a calm peace came over me. I knew the Lord was with me and that his words would flow from my mouth. That day the Lord cast His net of salvation and 120 students prayed to receive Jesus. It was a God moment forever branded in my heart. I do not know why God has allowed these things to happen in my life, but I am forever thankful. What I have learned is just to be AVAILABLE for the Lord Jesus to use you and He WILL!

Catawba S.C. 29704

I have had a great priviledge of knowing Brother Dave Walton for many years.
He has a tremendous passion and fire to share the grace and love of the Lord Jesus Christ.
I invited brother Dave on March 5-8 of 2006 for a revival at Roddey
Baptist Church .
During the morning hours, God opened a door for an opportunity to
speak at Metrolina Christian Academy at First Baptist Church of Indian
Trail in North Carolina.
To God be given all of the Glory, Pastor Dave spoke, gave an invitation
to accept Jesus Christ, and 120 decisions were made on that day.
Each of those students walked the aisle, and made a public confession.
Later that week, there were 4 decisions made at Winthrop College in
Rock Hill, SC, and then there was 1 precious soul saved at the Fort Mill Schools
in South Carolina.
There was also 1 decision at Shoneys Restaurant, and 9 decisions at Roddey Baptist Church in Catawba, SC during the revival there.

I praise Jesus Christ our Lord for using Brother Dave Walton in a great and mighty way.

Pastor Ronnie Helms

FELLOWSHIP OF CHRISTIAN ATHLETES
MR. WILL PACK

I asked my friend, Andrew to come and speak to our high school football team in Polk County, NC. With Andrew being a former two sport college athlete, I believed he would connect well with our players. As it turns out, Andrew was forced to go on a business trip and could not follow through with his commitment. Andrew offered to call his wife's uncle, Dave Walton to come and speak.

I wasn't familiar with Dave and so I was reluctant to have him come. After calling multiple people to come fill in and with no commitment, I called and asked Dave to come. He eagerly accepted the invitation.

With Dave being an older gentleman, I was wondering how he would relate to the players and how the players would accept what he had to say. When Dave showed up on that Friday afternoon, I could sense his passion for sports, football in particular, and Jesus. As Dave spoke to the team, the passion that I saw when we talked earlier was only magnified. Many of the same struggles and difficulties that he faced growing up are still issues in the lives of student-athletes today. His powerful testimony, through the power of the Holy Spirit, shot right through to the heart of everyone who was in that weight room on that Friday afternoon. 18 players indicated making a decision for Christ. Even through Andrew's business trip and my reluctance, God had a plan to use Dave to impact the Polk County football team and He fulfilled that plan.

- Will Pack, Polk and North Spartanburg FCA
Area Representative

Will Pack
Fellowship of Christian Athletes
Area Representative
North Spartanburg, SC/Polk County, NC

PASTOR VOLLIE GIBBS

Football is one of our greatest games in sports. It is full of life lessons that our young people will take with them for life. For many of our young boys, the coach becomes a father figure to them. Coach Kenny Lipsy is Ridge Spring Monetta's football coach. He is a man who teaches life principals, character, and the fundamentals of football.

Football camp began on the last Thursday of July (2016). The boys arrived at the gym at 6:00 pm to get ready for the first day of camp which started at 12:01 mid-night. After some bonding with team-mates and coaching, the team left and went to Mount Pleasant Baptist Church for a kick off Banquet meal and inspirational talk.

As the team chaplain, I invited one of my evangelist friend who was an outstanding football player at Spartanburg High back in his day. Brother Dave Walton shared his experiences as a quarterback and what it meant to be a leader of a football team. More importantly he shared his testimony and what it meant to be a Christian man and how Christ delivered him from alcohol and evil influences in his life. He spoke how Christians values can influence their performance both on and off the field. He challenged these young men to make a commitment to Jesus Christ, to set an example before their team-mates and peers. At the end of his testimony 10-15 young men responded unashamedly before their team-mates and coaches.

As a pastor, I have watched many young people respond to talks and challenges. Brother Dave Walton spoke with passion and gave such a strong personal and passionate plea to take a stand for Christ and become first a man of God and see what God would do if they remained true to their commitment. That evening I watched young men grow up and become leaders and followers of Christ.

These young returned to the gym excited and challenged to begin practice. At 12:01 the lights came on and practiced began. Yes it was football season again!!!!

Pastor Vollie Gibbs

Mount Pleasant Baptist Church

Ridge Spring, South Carolina

BE PREPARED

Most preachers love fried chicken and I have loved deep fried chicken ever sense I tasted my moms cooking. On this day I was very busy and in route to a meeting. As usual I was running a little late but something happen to me and my car as we passed BOJANGLES RESTAURANT. I felt I had time to go through the drive-thru and place an order for chicken and still make the meeting. A voice came over the intercom saying, may I take your order? Yes, I'll take a fried cygan filet chicken biscuit and diet soda.. She gave me the price and said drive forward to the first window. I gave the money for the order and I handed the cashier a tract and testified quickly. I was slowly pulling away and I heard a loud voice saying, please come back. I moved slowly backward to the ordering window and I heard these words. "My roommate and I were talking to each other this morning about how to be saved and we ask God to send someone who could explain how to receive eternal life," I said, "I am the man that God has sent!" There were no customers at the drive thru, so I knew God had closed the drive-thru for a moment so I could explain how to receive Jesus. I shared 30 sec testimomy quoting Romans 3:23, 6:23, 10:9-10. She said I am ready! Get the picture...at the cashier window praying the sinners prayer and Shelia received Jesus into her heart. It was SUPERNATURAL... God did it. It was a God setup. I give HIM all the praise

Bojangles Restaurant has become a good fishing hole for me. One morning as I headed to my prayer room I heard the LORD speak to my heart. HE said, "be prepared!" I was'nt sure what that meant but my heart went into alert mode. Several hours had pasted and I was out doing errands and I grew hungry. Well wouldn't you know, there is a Bojangles Restaurant and I think I have some fried chicken today. I went inside and ordered a meal and set down to enjoy some fried chicken. Then it happen, a school bus pulled into the restaurant parking lot and a lot of teens got off the bus and came inside the restaurant. In my heart I could hear the words, "be prepared." I started praying under my breath asking God what was I to do?" All the young teens I learned were basketball players and were headed for tournament play in the evening. All of a sudden the coach was standing at the soda fountain right beside me. I spoke to him and said, I played sports in high school but I made wrong decisions about life and it cost me 10 years of my life. Coach would you let me share with your team for about 5 minutes my sports story. He agreed and called his team together and ask them to listen to what I would say. THAT WAS SUPERNATURAL! Here I am in Bojangles sharing my testimony to a basketball team. Friend, that is just a God thing. After sharing my story I ask this team if there were any guys that wanted to become followers of Jesus. 9 team members prayed to receive Jesus in a Bojangles restaurant. That event was GOD SUPERNATURAL....

MY MOTIVATION FOR SOUL WINNING

I am motivated by God's love to be a soul winner. After receiving Jesus as my savior in 1975, something happened to me on the inside that caused me to be burdened for my lost loved ones, friends, and strangers. In 1975 my pastor encouraged me to pray and witness to people about eternal life. I started a 10 Most Wanted List of friends and loved ones, and I began to pray relentlessly, for them to come to a saving knowledge of Jesus Christ.

I remember some nights I could not sleep and instead, I prayed all night for their salvation. Day after day I would intercede for the deliverance of my friends who were held in bondage by Satan. I knew that God was going to answer my prayers.

In the meantime, I was a witness in the market place sharing Jesus with anyone who would listen to me. I became conscious of God's favor, power, and more aware of His presence with me, and on me, as I spoke.

On December 7, 1983, I had an encounter with God's Holy Spirit. It was a brokenness of heart that is impossible to describe. I was in prayer and all of a sudden I could hear cries of loved ones and friends weeping out loud, and they were crying for help. They were lost and headed for Hell; the place which is reserved for the Devil.

I was shaking all over and sweat ran down my face. A deep cry from within came forth asking God to fill me with boldness to witness. At that moment there was a fresh river of divine power flowing through me as I wept uncontrollably for lost souls. The anguish of prayer had hit its mark and from that day forward, the Lord has made me a "Fisher of Men".

Praying for lost souls and witnessing to lost people is always on my mind. Even today, I know there is a River of Living Water flowing out of my belly for lost souls. Just a few days ago I was telling my salvation story to a young man and he started crying. I saw that it was the Lord's conviction upon him and I knew the Lord was drawing him to salvation. I continued testifying and then I asked him if he desired to be a follower of Jesus. He said YES! He repented of his sins and asked Jesus to forgive him. Then, he invited Jesus into his heart. We shared a fulfilling God moment.

In my heart, I know that the Spirit of Jesus Christ is with me every moment, inspiring and fulfilling His assignments in my life. I must admit it is not always easy, but I am convinced that His power and presence are always with me.

The more I pray from the Secret Place, the more I see God with me, working through me, in the marketplace. I remain relentless at reaching people for the Kingdom of God. My example is Jesus. I am deeply moved as I read of Jesus on the cross. What is He doing with His last breath? Winning a thief to the Kingdom of God! This inspires and motivates me!

Joseph Caldwell

CEO of Consolidated Assurance

Few men have made such an impact on my life like Joseph Caldwell. We experienced mission trips together, dusty roads of evangelism in Nicaragua, laughter, hard work, and life as friends. I love his heart for the poor and his encouraging words to rekindle the fire of one's inner spirit. He is a loyal friend and a great partner with Dave Walton Ministries. He is a true blessing to my life! Joseph is a mighty warrior in business and a strong encourager to my life. (Judges 6:2)

MISSISSIPPI 1987

We traveled into Louisville, Mississippi in 1987 to the First Baptist Church for a weekend meeting with youth and adults. They called us Don and Dave the preaching deacons from SC., and we were fired up about sharing the power of Jesus and His love for the sinner to be set free. We shared the gospel Saturday and Sunday and Monday we were to fly home and then it happen!!!!

A teacher had met with the principle and the door had opened to speak before the entire school assembly. Only God! She was a member at First Baptist and was deeply moved by the testimonies of these two men and wanted the students to hear their message.

The minister of education and evangelism at the church said, " I had their clothes in the car to leave after school on Monday. But God had other plans as 500 students came forward at the end of the testimony making professions of faith."

God stirred the leaders of the church and they discussed what to do and agreed we should stay longer for unannounced revival. A call to the principle and the school auditorium was rented for the next two nights. Word got out and some 400 came each night to the school meetings with dozens of rededications and professions of faith recorded.

God rain down His glory and the meeting went into Supernatural mode! Schools like Nanih Wayih, Winston Academy, and Louisville Middle school recorded more than 1500 decisions for Jesus at the schools and church.

The principle at Nanih Wayih is also a deacon at Harmony Church. He said, he's been praying for something like this to happen at his school. He spoke to the students in his school over the loudspeaker saying that math is important, science is important, English is important....this is temporary, though, what you have heard today is eternal. God's love hit his school and students were receiving counsel because they were so broken. Then they just started loving on each other and asking for forgiveness. It was truly a God moment.

French camp got involved and started attending services with several profession of faith.

Another teacher offered to mail Bibles to any of her students whose home was without a Bible.We later learned she had mailed 40 Bibles.

The students said, we are covering Louisville with the love of Jesus. Students were being bold testifying in restaurants about being saved. It was SUPERNATURAL!

One student said, even the "wild" students are not the same. It was Supernatural. God pouring His love, forgiveness and mercy on those crying out to Him.

First Baptist leaders started sending out tracts and letters to all that responded to Jesus. They started a discipling class and a new Christian program called "Survival Kit" for new Christians.

When spiritual hunger cries out to God His presence overtakes a place. These youth were looking for the real Christianity and they found it in the true worship of Jesus Christ. I think they know now that Jesus does love them and He wants to give them the abundant life sais Pastor Cotton.

"WHEN SPIRITUAL HUNGER CRIES OUT TO GOD, HIS PRESENCE OVERTAKES A PLACE."

THE BALANCED LIFE

I have often heard pastors preach on the balanced life and I would shake my head and say to myself, "What is that and what does it look like?" As an evangelist called out by God I am always desiring to be somewhere preaching the gospel, doing mission work, visiting a prison, comforting someone in a nursing home, or one-on-one witnessing. It is hard for me to slow down…and one night it caught up with me.

I remember being on the evangelism trail hot and heavy and seeing many salvations. It seemed like I was gone all the time. I would come home to change clothes and head out the next day for a revival. This was my normal schedule for years. The opportunities for revivals grew to as many as 45 per year.

I arrived home from a revival to prepare for the next one. It became time to leave and I was telling everyone goodbye and how much I loved them. All of a sudden, as I was passing our daughter Holly, I stopped and took a look at her; really took a long pause and looked at her. She was growing up. My mind raced backward and I was standing there remembering her looking like a 9 year old, but now I was looking into the face of a 14 year old young woman.

Traveling the interstate to get to Chester, South Carolina I was still seeing the face of my teenager. Souls were in the balance and I had to get to Chester so they could be saved. Yet, somewhere along the highway something happened to me on the inside. I missed five years of my daughter's life.

The eruption in my heart was like a raging river, as my eyes flooded with tears and spilled over. I began crying so hard I thought I would die. I was near a nervous breakdown. Oh, you say, you were doing God's will, anointed of God to preach the gospel and win souls for Jesus. Yes, it is true, but <u>I think it may have become my God rather than God being my God.</u>

We made it to the revival and several more. One with Dr. Fred Wolfe and Cottage Hill Baptist in Mobile, Alabama. One look at me and he said, I looked like I needed a revival. I was run-down and had a heavy heart. **Brother Fred would help me see that time has to be taken off for family-time or I may not have a family, and thus, my ministry could be destroyed.** WOW! **What an eye opener!** He ministered to me. He schooled me in how to set up meetings and still have valuable family-time. His words and leadership saved my life and marriage.

He then said, "I am flying your family to Mobile and I am getting you a place to stay at Gulf Shores. I want you to rest and enjoy family-time and come preach revival at Cottage Hill Baptist only for evening services." God sent the right man into my life at the right time. He continues to mentor me in ministry and lifestyle. He taught me how to live a balanced life as I continue to serve the Lord.

DOOR TO DOOR IN NICARAGUA

I am praising God for the outstanding mission team I had this year in Nicaragua. At THE FLAGS community they served some 350 plates of food to the people who attended the REVIVAL. Leaders in the Flags community helped prepare the food. Praising JESUS! Altars filled with Nicaraguans wanting a transformed life. The love our team showed to the people made the difference. Across the road from the church our team built a home for the youth minister and his wife and I wish you could have been there and seen the great smiles on their face. "SO GRATEFUL!" Edgar Mendoza and Nathan Wells and Joseph Caldwell worked hard to complete project in 2 days. Our team went door to door to evangelize the community and many received Jesus. The week of sharing Jesus was fruitful as 99 people made professions of faith. We then traveled to Mt. Sion Church and conducted a 2 day revival. God was with us. A singing group was birthed from our team and they were awesome. Isabella, Madelyn, Cameo, Mellissa, and Jaden brought the house down as they sang during REVIVAL. The church love it! A final note!!!! Our team passed out 26 YELLOW BAGS that contained shoes and clothing (uniform) so that these students could start to school. It was a very moving GOD moment. ~~Thanks to all who gave.~~
~~16. JESUS IS LORD!~~

Nehemiah 4:6
So build we the wall: and all the wall was joined together unto the half thereof: for the people had a mind to work

"That at the name of Jesus every knee should bow" Philippians 2:10

MUDDY ROAD LEADS TO CLEAN HEARTS

This mission trip was special. We would have to endure rain, mud, and heat. The bus carrying us pulled of the main road to a side road. We could not go any further in the bus because of the mud. Many church members were waiting for us at the Emanuel Church and we needed to make a decision. Our Nicaraguan leader ask if we wanted to come back at a better time or walk in the mud for about a quarter of a mile to the church. In one accord the team started walking in the rain and mud to the church. When we arrived the church was overflowing with people and the joy of the Lord hit the place when the Nicaraguans saw us coming. Souls were saved that night! For two days we walked in mud and rain to present the gospel of Jesus and the ladies on our team went door to door witnessing to people about Jesus in ankle deep mud. Again more souls were saved.

Meanwhile the men were working in the rain and mud on a new home for Associate Pastor Francisco. This team had come to Nicaragua with fire in their heart to do the work. It took two days but the team completed a new home with shower and outhouse for the pastor. I was so proud of Pastor Mike, Jamie, Pastor D, Edgar, Reggie and Joseph for the extra work poured into this project. To God be the glory!

On to Xiola Barrio where the ladies on the team (Diane,Missy,Brooke, Alexandra, and Sue, would do a program for the school children and the men did a soccer match with the young men of the barrio. Again the Lord was faithful in giving us many souls for our labor. On to The Flaggs Barrio which is a new work, and the people living here were poor and hungry with very little housing. Our team went right to work providing 147 bags of groceries and repairing three homes and providing some 300 sweet rolls for the children. The gospel was shared and souls were saved. The muddy road, the rain, the heat, yes it was difficult but in the end 137 souls were saved. Praise Jesus! Special thanks to all who provided the money for the projects and food. We are eternally grateful!

SOUTHSIDE LETTER PAGE 1

Southside Baptist Church

1201 Highway 26, West, Lucedale, MS 39452 Ph. 601-947-3136

TOM MILLER, Pastor

May 28, 1992

Acts 3:19 was a Scripture cited as a theme for my heart as we were making preparation for the coming of Don & Dave. We had prayed much that God would pour His spirit upon us. The deacons had cottage prayer meetings in their homes. We erected a tent that would seat more people than our sanctuary. We felt the excitement of anticipation through each phase of preparation. On Wednesday one week prior to the coming of the team we met for setting goals. There was a hesitancy on the part of the church. I was sure I had heard God that 100 souls would be reached for Jesus. I wrote this on the overhead and I announced it at every meeting. I first felt a caution about stating 100 souls but with each announcement it became more real. I came to not have any doubt whatsoever.

I visited the High School principle and gained approval to speak to a portion of the student body in the cafeteria. Two separate hours were set and I was disappointed when I was told 120 would be in each group. I later asked our church to pray that this would change. I called two prison facilities and gained access to one. Had I been a little more open I could have gotten into the second. I must admit that I was hesitant to contact other schools. But this was to change.

When Sunday arrived people were excited but this was just a trickle. I was thrilled by then because God had confirmed many expectations. After Sunday services a teacher who normally doesn't step out at school on occasions like this said she would speak to her principal but, he wasn't too responsive to such requests. Lo and behold! he allowed an opportunity but no invitation could be given. This was at our middle school. we spoke to over 450 students. Don had every eye and heart.

The High School moved the meeting place to the gymnasium and had air conditioning on. We had 2 groups of over 450. The attention of the students so impressed the High School Guidance Counselor that she was amazed. When we saw this acceptance we took another step of faith giving an invitation that called for students to come forward for prayer. The bleachers emptied! Many had raised their hands saying they were making first time decisions. I estimated over one hundred from the two High School groups. Praise the Lord! Youth night students came and publicly professed Jesus as savior.

A mother pleaded with me to call the Elementary school closest to us. The principle was excited about it. I called another middle school and that principle said, yes! Unbelievable. Then they allowed an invitation, Hallelujah! we saw the previous numbers triple. We saw over 2000 students and my most unexaggerated estimates are that over 400 first time decisions and 1600 commitments to make a difference for Jesus.

SOUTHSIDE LETTER PAGE 2

We later went to the prison and I was astounded at the freedom to preach that was there! Sixteen precious souls came to Jesus. I was excited we had the last night of revival I had expected more to attend and we had announced for people to bring lawn chairs. Some people did. We had a full tent. Lives and marriages were rekindled for the service of God that night. After the dust settled we had 53 cards that recorded salvation.

On Sunday I presented a video recording of the invitations at the schools and we baptized eight and we will baptize again next week. I had a leak in my waders and got soaked and had to change clothes. Then when I reached to turn off a light it shocked me. I told the congregation that the devil wasn't going to steal my joy, praise God!

This week following the revival many people have spoken of the renewal they sensed and they were not members of our church. When sharing with our church the comments, they verify that these people were very unlikely to say anything, muchless to speak positive of such an event.

I could go on and on but let me stop here and say that Don and Dave have been greatly used of God here. They were supportive of the church and it's pastor. They challenged both to a closer walk with God. I have a renewed vision and hunger for the things of God and the plans He has for His church. Don and Dave appeal to other church in our area of different denominations. Yet, they never acted or strayed away from the beliefs of our church or any sister Southern Baptist Church.

Don and Dave are recommended to you by me and Southside Baptist Church unreservedly to act responsibly and never to bring reproach upon a church or pastor in any way. I encourage prayerful consideration of this team as they are mightily used of God. I also was conscious of Ephesians 3:20 that God will do exceeding abundantly above all that we ask or think...and praise the Lord He did!

In His service,

Tom

Tom Miller, Pastor
Southside Baptist Church

WHAT THEY SAID

Dr. Fred Wolfe, Pastor Emeritus
Cottage Hill Baptist Church
Mobile, Alabama

Dave Walton is a powerful preacher of God's word. His messages are Biblically based and applied to daily life. He will bless your church.

Dr. Michael S. Hamlet, Sr.
First Baptist North Spartanburg
Spartanburg, South Carolina

Dave Walton has a tremendous heart for lost people. His greatest desire is to serve the Lord and to see people come to know Christ through the presentation of the gospel.

Evangelist Junior Hill

"Over these many years of being a traveling preacher, I have met hundreds of men and women with a passion to win the lost - but very, very few with the intensity of Dave Walton. He is a man on fire for Jesus! He lives and breathes soul-winning. If you want a man who will come to your church and build a fire of evangelism in your fellowship I would encourage you to invite Dave. You will be glad that your did and your church will be blessed."

LIBERTY BAPTIST CHURCH

I've never known anyone more zealous to win souls to Christ than Evangelist Dave Walton. He reminds me of a biblical prophet with his anointed ability to stir the people of God out of complacency to new levels of complete surrender to the Lord Jesus Christ. I commend him to any pastor seeking someone who is bold enough to confront their church with God's truth and challenge them to live accordingly.

Brother Dave was recently with us for a crusade and the results were amazing. In three area schools we saw dozens of young people give their lives to Christ. I commend him without any reservation whatsoever.

Pastor Owen Duncan

"Dave Walton is one of the best Youth Communicators I know. Our students really connect with his preaching. Dave's love for students and challenging messages have made an incredible impact on our Student Ministry. We can't wait to have him back."
Shawn Doss, Minister of Students - Mount Vernon Baptist Church

Hi Dave, Sorry I have been quite busy this past week. I am still hearing a lot of praises about our revival. You know we had more than 30 people saved during the revival services. I have been pastoring for 40 years and the last time I remember having a revival like we had was back in the late 1960's. I have had many so called revivals but nothing like we experienced here at The Chapel in the Woods. It was more than just people getting saved. The Christians were brought into a deeper relationship to our Lord and as a result they are now hungering for more of God in their lives. They want to see souls saved and added to His Kingdom. We are still preparing and planning for our next revival in October. Can't wait for you to return for the fall revival. Rev. Jerry Brunson

Dr. Robbie Howand
First Baptist Church Helena
Moss Point, Mississippi

I have known Dave Walton for nearly twenty years. During that time, I have been with him in various evangelistic endeavors. In every situation, Dave has manifested a deep love and concern for the unsaved. He is a true soldier of the cross. If the Lord leads you to use him for any type of outreach, you will be fully blessed.

From Your Director of Missions

Recently I had the opportunity to attend a very exciting revival service at the FBC Cleveland, Dave Walton from Spartanburg, South Carolina was the revival speaker. The service was wonderful and the fellowship was great. The evangelist made a strong evangelistic appeal. All this was preceded by a song service led by Chris Green. During the invitation there were so many professions of faith that you were either at the altar getting saved or were down from leading someone to Christ. What at first seemed like a typical revival service, suddenly turned into something truly blessed by God. In all there were 34 professions of faith and of those 26 have followed through in believers baptism. Praise the Lord, I would encourage all our churches to schedule a revival this summer as a follow up to VBS.

PREACHING FROM A SCHOOL BUS

I am exited and rejoice with you that your prayers ~~[illegible]~~s are making a tremendous difference in this Soul-Winning Ministry.

Last year we watched God move on hearts and saw a harvest of over a 1000 souls. We had several called out into Christian service in our meetings. I have also learned that two young men were called into the pastorate. Now that sets my heart on fire.

Remember…our ministry is all about SOULS !!!! I remain dedicated to winning souls and proclaiming the Gospel of Jesus Christ to every man, woman, and child who will listen. We are seeing REAL RESULTS with REAL PEOPLE who have REAL NEEDS in their lives. You help bring a SAVING message to this HURTING world.

I just got home from a mission trip to Nicaragua where we saw many salvations, served 1200 hot meals to needy children, built 4 homes and 4 out houses and gave some 300 bags of groceries to needy church families. WOW !!! It was a GOD thing.

~~In close pl~~ease remember that the harvest fields are ripe in Nicaragua, American Schools, and Prisons. Our revivals in America are incredible as we see the LORD saving many souls.

~~Thank you again for STANDING with us.~~ Yo~~u will never know just how thankful I am that you are there~~! I remain on the front lines for JESUS winning one soul at a time!!!

Dave

Something new… Preaching from a school bus…

FRANK SHIVERS

531 MOTIVATIONS FOR WINNING SOULS WRITES OF DAVE WALTON

114 Dave Walton's Motivation

Dave Walton is an exemplary soul winner. Walton shares, "On September 7, 1975, I came to salvation through the prayers of a man who had fasted and prayed for me. I immediately became strongly involved with the church where I met Jesus. Pastor Rupert Guest was always challenging his congregation to pray and witness.

"It was at this time that I developed my first 10 Most Wanted List. My heart was burdened for my lost loved ones and friends. I began to pray with faith, believing that these that I was praying for would be saved. This pushed me into being a faithful intercessor. In due time, I became conscious of God's favor and power and presence with me.

"On December 7, 1983, I had an encounter with God's Holy Spirit. It was a brokenness of heart that is impossible to describe. I was in prayer, and all of a sudden, I could hear the cries of loved ones and friends crying for help. These were lost and headed to a Devil's Hell. In that moment, there was a fresh river of divine power flowing through me as I wept out of control for lost souls. The anguish of prayer had hit its mark. From that day forward, the Lord has made me a 'Fisher of Men.'

"From that day even until now there is a River of Living Water flowing out of my belly for lost souls. In my heart, I know that the Spirit of Jesus Christ is with me every moment, inspiring and fulfilling His assignments in my life. It is not always easy, but I am convinced that His power and presence are always with me.

"The more I pray from the secret place, the more I see God with me in the marketplace as I share my personal salvation story. I remain relentless at reaching people for the Kingdom of God. My example is Jesus. I am deeply moved as I read of Jesus on the Cross. What is He doing with His last breath? Winning a thief to the Kingdom of God. This inspires and motivates me to do the same."[194]

---

[193] Ibid., 491–492.

[194] Walton, Personal Correspondence, March 27, 2010.

Frank Shivers has been in vocational evangelism since 1974 and is a member both of his State and National Conference of Southern Baptist Evangelists. He is a graduate of Charleston Southern University (BA) and the New Orleans Baptist Theological Seminary (Th.M). Frank has authored thirteen books including *Soul Winning 101* which cites 275 helps in winning the lost to Christ and *Growing in Knowledge, Living by Faith: An Interactive Handbook on Basic Christian Truths*. In addition to conducting crusades, revivals, and evangelistic rallies, Frank hosts student camps and retreats at Longridge Camp and Retreat Center, Ridgeway, South Carolina, a facility owned and operated by his ministry. Frank lives in Columbia, South Carolina, with his wife, Mary.

SOUTH AFRICA
MISSION UPDATE PAGE 1

God sent me to South Africa. Before I left I called John Wilton who was a pastor there for years. He was kind enough to give me some wisdom of the area I would be staying and also to pray for me. I left on Friday April 30 for a 24 hour flight with stops at Detroit, Amsterdam, and then Cape town, South Africa. We would stay at Fish Hoek for the first week of revivals. I like the name Fish Hoek. God has called me to be a "Fisher of Men," and I want to be found faithful. Three of us worked the streets of Fish Hoek for several days. God was faithful in giving us some souls for our labor. Edgar Mendoza was on fire telling his story to anyone who would listen. I saw several cashiers in stores and men on the streets bow their heads and pray for Christ to change their lives. One young man was Shawn that the gospel was given to on the streets. He was educated and well mannered and the Lord's conviction fell upon him. It was marvelous to see the working of the Holy Spirit on him in the streets of Fish Hoek. I saw a store clerk overcome with the compassion of the Spirit weeping and asking us "how do I get saved." We knew the Lord was with us!
I spoke at the Full Gospel Church on Sunday morning May 2. They were not too sure of me because of being a Baptist. Yet about 2 minutes into the meeting the Holy Spirit moved into the place of worship as I preached with fresh fire from heaven on me. At one time the entire church from the balcony down was standing and praising God. His glory had overtaken us. People begin to weep out of control. I gave an altar call and 13 came forward for salvation. Spontaneous voices were crying out "I love you Jesus." It is hard to describe the effect of this upon the men. The men of the congregation made a rush to the altar and begin to repent. I got out of the way and watched in amazement the working of the Holy Spirit. To God be the glory!
Monday night May 3, I spoke at Bethel Evangelistic Band also known as Bethel Work. They have been involved in Evangelism in South Africa and Namibia since 1945. Students are trained at Bethel Bible School for full-time work in the ranks of the FEB. I was there by the invitation of Pastor Claude Van Graan. He is a tireless worker for the Lord God. He has been raising up young champions for the Lord for 27 years. The worship music set the tone for the meeting. The young people handled the music and the Lord was with them. I preached on the word "LOST." God moved as 8 young people came to Christ.
Tuesday night May 4, It was raining like cats and dogs. It was a frog stinger. I said to the pastor," In America this would be night that not many would come to services." At 7pm our service time to start the church was packed. I could hardly believe my eyes. Pastor said that many had come from an hours drive and many walked in the rain to get to the

SOUTH AFRICA MISSION UPDATE PAGE 2

services. Joy filled the house as the young people begin to sing the praises of God. It was truly a God moment for me as 13 more prayed to receive Christ that night. After services we went over to Pastor Claude's home. We had some tea with the family and several of the evangelistic workers. All of a sudden they begin to sing unto the Lord. It was an awesome moment as the Lord showed up and ministered to us. Then a prayer meeting broke out. I was really ministered to. Thank you Jesus!

Wednesday night May 5. Tonight there was great expectation in the service. Many brought their friends with them. That night the Lord lead me to ask everyone to bow their heads and pray for a lost friend or love one. We then begin to call their names out loud in the congregation(first name only). It is hard to describe the atmosphere of the place at that time. Worship hit a high level and people came forward and carried the names of the love ones to the altar. Salvations were happening everywhere. The Lord's house was filled with HIS LOVE. Praise the Lord!

During the days of this week I was taken to homes and there I shared my story with many people. William a gardener, Iris a street cleaner, Gideon a student, Viliam a lodge owner, Renee a prison guard, and others came to know Jesus as their Lord and Savior.

Thursday May 6 started the Heart Cry Conference for South Africa in Worchester,South Africa. I turned 63 on this day in S. Africa. The conference was awesome as we heard Sammy Tippet preach. Many lives were changed.

Friday May 7 I went to Breede River Prison in Worchester. I was to speak to the ladies division. Chaplin Andrew would escort me to this area of the prison. I found out that 80% of these women had killed their husbands because of abuse. I preached on "The love of the Father." God sent the River of love through that prison and women weep in great repentance. I had never seen it on this fashion. God showed himself faithful and full of mercy to these women. Many lives were changed.

Saturday May 8, I spoke at the "assisted living home." Now this was a treat. They came in their finest clothes. I preached on " The Reality of His Coming. 10 more come into the Kingdom of God. I had to stay late because they wanted to talk and hug one another including me. It was awesome!

May 9-12, I am with Pastor Ruben outside of Paarl, South Africa. He is a very powerful preacher in his own right and the Lord has gifted him with a great singing voice. His son played the key board with a strong anointing. I preached on "I am not ashamed of the gospel." This week we would see 23 salvations. Let me tell you about Tuesday night. I preached from ISA. 43:18-19. This message was hitting hard and the Holy Spirit was at work. Right in the middle of my message a man fell over and cried with a loud voice. He was shaking and crying out of control. The church members stood and raised their hands toward him and prayed. I later learned that this man had been a backslidden evangelist for 6 years. Tonight he was coming home. I later learned that Pastor Ruben had begged him to come to a service. To God be the glory!

5/26/2010

SOUTH AFRICA
MISSION UPDATE PAGE 3

HEART CRY FROM SOUTH AFRICA

We have been busy about our Father's business. In South Africa we conducted several revivals and visited the prisons and schools and assisted living homes. We are plundering hell to populate heaven for Calvary's sake. The impact of the Gospel is eternal, and we saw the working of the Holy Spirit everywhere we went in South Africa. From Allendale Prison we saw men crying out for the Lord Jesus. When the dust settled we did one on one prayer with the inmates. I saw harden men break under the love of God. Robin Spengler a member of CMA and Prison Ministry Coordinator for us got several doors open to the prisons to share Christ. I was touched deeply as I spoke to the women at Worchester Prison. God broke our hearts as well as the women inmates. Many trusted in Jesus for salvation.

NOTHING CAN RESHAPE LIFE LIKE FAITH IN GOD

Following Christ changes individuals, which reform cities and alters the course of nations. We saw revival break out in Worchester, Wellington, and Paarl. The Fire Conference in Worchester brought hundreds to Christ. Angus Buchan was the main speaker who has written a book on "The story of a farmer who risked everything for God." His book "faith like potatoes" has been made into a film. In 2009, (500,000) men gathered on his farm to pray and repent and cry out for revival in South Africa. I hope you will get the book and read it.

SOUTH AFRICAN PRISON

Matthew 25:36 I was in prison and you visited me.

I have had the opportunity to visit many prisons and share my testimony. I remember traveling with J. T. Cooper and his wife for several years into Tyger correctional and Broad River Correctional in South Carolina. God was faithful in helping us reach many inmates.

Recently I have been traveling with Jon Simone of Promised Land Prison Ministry into Tyger Correctional, and Foothills Correctional in Morganton North Carolina. I believe a great revival is coming forth from the prison house of suffering. Many men are repenting of their sins and calling on Jesus for salvation.

In 2010, I conducted several revivals in South Africa over a 16-day period. The leaders of this revival trip asked if I would speak in a prison while I was there and I accepted. I spoke to the ladies division of the prison and many accepted Jesus.

One of the most incredible opportunities to speak in prison was in Nicaragua. Guillermo Morales, on staff with Chosen Children Ministries, knew the warden and the meeting was to be arranged...provided we served a hot cooked meal to the inmates, who would attend. We made up some zip lock bags with hygiene products for the inmates, too.

This prison had about 3000 inmates. We would only be allowed to speak to 76 of the toughest in this prison. The warden said, "You will have guards with you as you will be locked behind bars in a large cell with these inmates. Your team will feed them first and then you can share your testimony."

Into the cell block we went, walking down a concrete hallway until we arrived at cell holding number 3. Directly across from cell 3 were men crying out for help and asking if we were going to provide food for them. I learned that those men received one meal a day, and one cup of coffee a day. There were no beds, no bathrooms, and no showers in this prison. One inmate said, "We take a bath once a day." He pointed to a small PVC pipe coming from the wall above and described, "The water runs out once a day and we gather together like a herd of animals and take a bath". He then pointed to a six inch circle in the floor and told us, "This is our bathroom."

I knew I was in prison and to be honest I was somewhat fearful even though we had 10 guards with us. The warden got the inmates to line up against the wall and come one at a time for a plate of rice, beans, chicken and some vegetables. Hungry men, not even taking time to eat with a fork, used their hands. I saw hurting men, men depressed, men with no hope, almost like animals, yet I knew God had us there for a purpose.

After all the inmates had eaten a hot cooked meal the warden had them sit on the concrete floor and he said to them, "Listen to what these men have to say because it could change your life."

I asked Edgar Mendoza to testify, then Ricky Cochran, and then I closed the meeting with scripture and a sermon. I was totally prepared with the message and had memorized scripture for this event.

As I began to speak there were 5 guards on my left and 5 guards on my right. The warden stood behind me. Words began to flow from my mouth and I felt I had the right message. Then, suddenly, the Lord changed course in my spirit to share about my Mom and her up-bringing, and how she accepted Jesus. Then I shared how I broke my Mother's heart doing evil and how my Mother loved me through the tough times in my life.

The Lord's presence was strong and I could see the eyes of several inmates and there were tears streaming down their faces. The Lord had directed the message to the heart of the matter for these men. A Mother praying and weeping for her son and daughter is a beautiful thing and so it was this day in this Nicaraguan prison as 27 hard core inmates received Jesus.

It is a God moment forever branded into my heart.

My friend, you may have a loved one serving time in a prison, but know this, God is on the move in prisons and inmates are coming to know Jesus because men of God are visiting the prison house of suffering. I encourage you to pray for inmates.

Thank you!

REV. JON SIMONE'S PRISON MINISTRY

I don't know how to explain it, but the Holy Spirit seemed to say to my heart, "vacation is over and you are needed in the North Carolina prison." I had to obey! We cut our vacation short to go home and go to Morganton, North Carolina, to be a part of Rev. Jon Simone's prison outreach at Foothills Correctional Institute.

I have been to Foothills Correctional Institute several times and preached, but in my heart I knew something different was about happen. Sunday rolled around and Diane and I went to church and Bible Fellowship and we had lunch together. Diane departed for home and I sat in my car praying for the LORD to have His way at the prison crusade. It is July 3rd and many folk are heading for their short July 4th weekend vacation.

The church bus arrived for us to load and head to the prison. I said to myself, "there are some young people I don't recognize going with us." I would later meet them and learn that they would be the music for the prison crusade. I remember going to the back of the bus and preparing my heart for more prayer. The trip to Morganton, North Carolina, is about an hour and forty-five minutes from First North Church; during that time I heard the LORD say to me, "release." I knew what that meant, so I began to run Bible stories across my mind. My first thought was Stephen being stoned to death in the book of Acts. The second story came as fast as the first and it was Jesus on the cross dying. Both of these Bible stories have Stephen and Jesus ask forgiveness for those that are killing them. In other words they forgave their killers. Each one said, "Forgive them."

This is so powerful. I have learned that one must release those that have hurt them. In doing so it gives freedom to the one releasing. Well we travelled on into Morganton and I was just waiting on the Holy Spirit to give me direction.

Then it happened!

Then Rocc Reggie was introduced and he is an anointed rapper. WOW, he stunned the inmates with his music and powerful testimony. God was in the house and we all knew God was about to do something.

Jon Simone of Promise Land Prison Ministry looked at me and said, "God told me you have a word for tonight."

Dave Walton and Rev. Jon Simone

I preached on the power of "release." You have to forgive people and don't carry bitterness around toward someone. Release the guilt, release the burden, and release those who have hurt you, and release that thing that keeps you in the devil's grip and be free. Let freedom ring in your heart. It happened to me as I forgave my accusers and started praying for them and the most amazing thing happen to me. God filled me with His fire to preach the gospel and that night 35 inmates prayed to receive Jesus.

That's GOD. To Him be all the glory!

I want to thank the team of volunteers that travelled into Morganton July 3, because your faithfulness and prayers made an eternal difference in many inmates' lives. Special thanks for all those who provided donuts and lemonade for the inmates. Together we have made an eternal difference in some hurting lives.

Brother Jon is a powerful preacher,

seeing over 3000 inmates come to

Jesus in 2016.

I am humbled that he would open

the door for me to speak to the inmates.

Tipitapa Trash Dump

Several years ago, *Chosen Children Ministries* took me to the trash dump in Nicaragua and it changed my life forever. I could smell the trash burning and the air filled with smoke and odours of rotten food. Vultures (scavenging birds) flew all over the ground searching for food. Trash was everywhere you looked and people, young and old, searched in the trash dump for food to eat or some treasure to sale in hopes to purchase food. I saw it with my own eyes, families with little children digging through the trash.

The trash dump is not too far from the prison in Tipitapa. I had been there once and preached to the inmates who live in very difficult circumstances. I do not have the words to describe what I saw. As I stood on a hill at the dump, I could see trucks loaded with trash coming and the people were hanging on the trucks waiting to get the trash that would be dumped into a seventy-foot hole. Smoke poured out of this hole but the people didn't seem to care.

Hunger has a way of making you do things that are dangerous and unhealthy. I talked to some of the people in the trash dump and found them to be humble and thankful for life. They did not complain about being there; but did say to me that they wished their children could have a better life than trying to survive in a trash dump.

Now, for the rest of the story!

We did not have the power or the resources to change such a dire situation, but we can do something. This makes me so proud of working with *Chosen Children Ministries* and helping the poor of Nicaragua. CCM is now providing clothing, shoes, and school material for the children to go to school. We know that an education is important to advance in this world. Like we did, most mission teams going into the trash dump, and carry groceries to help meet the food need. It is an ongoing process but CCM is making a difference and we are most honored to be a part.

My wife and I were burdened, not only for the food needs, but we knew that these wonderful people needed spiritual guidance. We prayed for God to show us *what* to do. A very short distance from the trash dump is a church called Crystal Rey and God moved on us to build a new church there, so we could help support the families living in the trash dump.

I can report to you that many lives are being changed and many mission teams going to the trash dump are also making a significant difference in these families' lives. Only God could orchestrate these happenings and we are so thankful to be a small part.

We extend our special thank you to the partners of Dave Walton Ministries who made this possible, and our great partnership with *Chosen Children Ministries* in Nicaragua.

TREE STUMP PREACHING

I have read books on the ole time preachers who stood on tree stumps and preached revivals in an open air meeting. A creek bank, river bank, it didn't bother them. The 25,000 who came to Cane Ridge Prayer Meeting years ago listened to a preacher as he preached from a tree stump.

Our mission team was in Nicaragua and we were looking for a new community to possibly start a church. We went visiting door to door and invited everyone to one of the community leader's home to talk about a new church. To our amazement a large crowd gathered outside the leader's home and the number of people kept growing.

J. T. and Barbara Cooper were with me on this mission trip. We had been doing a lot of prison ministry together in South Carolina. J. T. Cooper said, "I have a great idea." He said, "Dave, do you see that tree stump about 20 yards from us? You need to go and stand on that stump and preach the good news of Jesus Christ to all these folks who have walked here to learn about a new church."

I asked Guillermo Morales to interpret for me and he agreed. Guillermo is a leader of Chosen Children Ministries in Nicaragua. They helped me get up on the stump and the Lord filled me with a message of hope. I shared about Paul in the Bible and how he was locking up Christians and putting them in jail. I told them how Jesus called him to preach the gospel of Jesus while traveling on the Damascus road. I shared my story of alcohol and my life of unforgiveness toward others.

The Lord showed up and people began to cry. Many people came forward at the time of invitation. They gathered around that stump and prayed to be saved. It was a God moment for me and I treasure that event in my life.

TRASH DUMP PREACHING

In Nicaragua I have learned to be ready at all times to preach, and so it was as we were giving out food to the families at the trash dump. Everyone was given a bag of rice, beans, cooking oil, and spices for several meals. I just state, “Let me have a few moments with you and I will tell you my story.” I used Romans 1: 16 and shared that for many years I was not a Christian, until a man fasted and prayed over my soul. He invited me to church and that is how I heard the good news that Jesus loved me.

As I was preaching, I heard the Lord speak to my heart saying, “Walk among them and hug them. Keep telling them of my love for them.” I had never done anything like this in my life. As I would preach, I hugged people and it was amazing to see them weep. Many cried out to be saved and be followers of Jesus. God took some trash out their hearts and turned them into treasured hearts.

One young teenager was crying uncontrollably. The Nicaraguans called me over to pray for him. He was very dirty because he had been digging in the trash for food and clothes. He was smelly, and the stench of burning trash was on his dirty clothes. His tears rolled down his face and you could see the trail of tears through the dirt on his face. My heart cried out for Jesus to help me.

I heard the Lord say to me, in my heart, “Hug him.” I did hug him and something happened to him and to me. Jesus was with us at that moment, as we embraced, and we both knew it. All of a sudden, I felt like I was hugging Jesus. The stench began to smell good, as this young man surrendered his life to Jesus. What an incredible day at the trash dump. My lie was changed, forever. I have learned to simply love people; for it is the one thing we all need...HIS LOVE!

FLAG RIVER

Matthew 28: 19 "Go ye therefore and make disciples of all nations, baptizing them in the name of the Father, and the Son, and the Holy Spirit."

Baptism is a very important first step of obedience after becoming a Christian. I have been doing mission work in Nicaragua for 12 years with Wallace and Kim Nix from Chosen Children Ministries. At Flag River I had the opportunity to baptize.

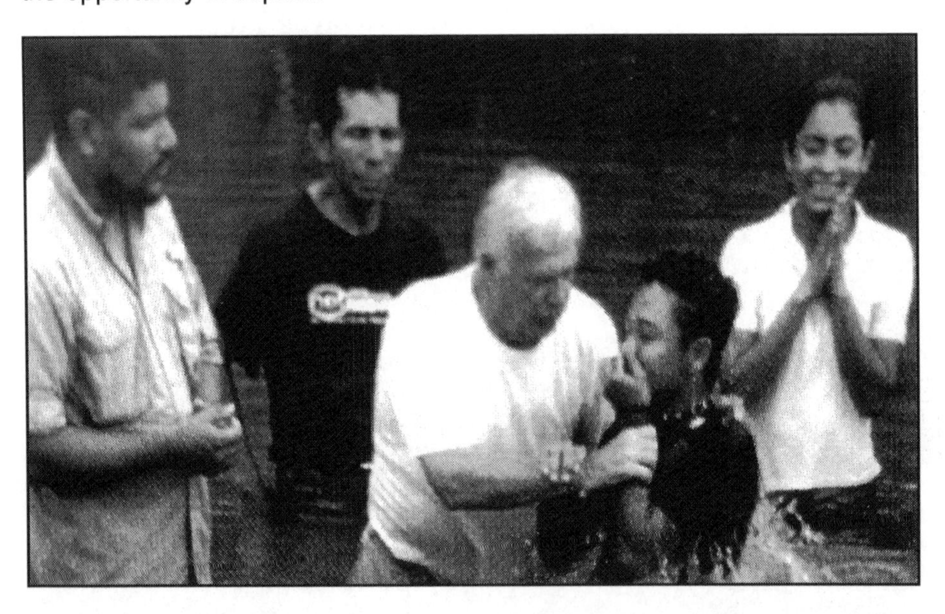

This moment is frozen, like time standing still, forever in my heart. I look back in time and wonder why God would allow me to have so many wonderful God moments. I can this moment in my mind's eye now, as I type this story.

I had conducted several revivals in communities where we had the opportunity to be a part of building churches. Upon arrival to the church the pastor asked me to baptize the new converts, where I had preached revivals. Pastor Francisco said 27 were ready. We used one of the CCM busses and traveled to Flag River. The bus holds 45, but that was filled, and refilled again! The Nicaraguan's take baptism seriously. When we left the bus, we traveled a wide path down to the riverbank. Guillermo Morales asked those being baptized to walk into the river, all 27 of them. As we did, everyone remaining on the river's bank began singing Amazing Grace. It was an incredible God moment that I will never forget. I was humbled by this experience and very grateful they wanted me to baptize them.

I fell in love with the Nicaraguan church and their God-fearing pastors. They are true worshippers of the Lord of Host and they inspire me to give it all I got in the harvest fields for the Lord.

Thank you Wallace and Kim Nix of Chosen Children Ministries for the tireless efforts you put into our Nicaragua Mission trips!

JACK RHODEHAMEL

MR. JACK RHODEHAMEL

Upon graduation from high school I enrolled at Spartanburg Methodist College. At the same time, I was hired by Mr. Jack Rhodehamel to head up the athletic department of the Salvation Army's Red Shield Boys Club. It was located on William Street. Jack became a mentor to me, showing me the way the army did things. Their goal was to work with young people in hopes of keeping them off the streets and out of trouble. I was battling alcohol problems, but Jack worked with me and it did a lot of good.

My coaching skills were not up to par and my Dad would come and watch me coach so he could give me pointers to better lead. Early into practice, one day, my Dad asked me, "Who are your running backs?" I answered, "I don't know, Daddy." He replied, "Want some help deciding?" I asked him, "How would I figure out who the running backs should be?" He said, "Let the team race for a hundred yards, and the boys that cross the finish line first are your running backs, and wide receivers. The slower ones are your linemen." Pretty smart I thought. I used that technique for several years. I coached some great athletes of which some became football stars in high school. Some went on to play pro ball.

Jack Rhodehamel was the most loving man I have ever met. He was a family man and fought tooth and nail for the kids at the Red Shield Boys Club. His work ethic was hustle and hustle more for the kids. He would spend his own money to make sure lives were touched for the glory of God. Every child there knew that Mr. Rhodehamel loved them, and they loved him.

As life has it, it became time for me to move on and I entered Limestone College to get my BA Degree. I finished school in 1972. Years would pass and I learned of Jack's illness. I visited with him on several occasions and we would talk about old times. The last time I visited him was in a nursing home and he was in a lot of pain. I pulled a chair beside him and tried to talk to him, but he was in too much pain to carry on a conversation.

All of a sudden I heard in my heart a voice say, pray for him and hold his hand. I did just as I had heard! As I was praying, my mind was filled with many great thoughts and memories of Jack and our time together at the boys club. I bent over and kissed his head and kept on praying. As I finished praying he became quiet.

As I was singing out loud, the receptionist said to me, "I am sorry you had to be here while Mr. Rhodehamel was in such pain and screaming." I replied, "Lady, this man is a giant in my life, and for me to have a precious prayer time with him is really more than I could ever dream of. Just to be with him for a short time has been a major blessing."

I departed from the nursing home and would hear later that Jack had been promoted to Heaven. He was God's man on the earth and he was a true soldier of the Cross of Jesus Christ.

Thank you, Jack Rhodehamel, for believing in me when I could not believe in myself.

Week of Broadcast	Program #	Title	Topic
January 17 - 23, 1999	2509	Kevin Mazur	Alcohol/Loneliness
January 24 - 30, 1999	2510	Ralph Brooker	Alcohol-Classic
Jan. 31 - Feb. 6, 1999	2511	John Hauff	Bank Robbery/Electric Chair
February 7 - 13, 1999	2512	Dave Walton	Sports/Alcohol

UNSHACKLED RADIO SHOW

It was 1998 and I had just gotten off the phone with Flossie McNeil from the Pacific Garden Mission in Chicago, Illinois. She called me to ask me if I would consider giving my sports testimony on the *Unshackled* radio program. This radio program has been on the air since 1950. It airs programs dramatizing testimonies of people who have come to the saving knowledge of Jesus.

I was shocked and humbled at the same time, wondering "why me?" Flossie McNeil said to me, "*Unshackled* is looking for a sports story like yours to air on our program because it will speak to a lot of athletes around the world." I told her that, "I am overwhelmed and will do the program.

I thought this would be easy but I learned that *Unshackled* uses a live audience and actors act your testimony on radio. It is taped and then sent out to radio stations around the world.

I was mailed a form to fill out and it took me days to answer all the questions. They also wanted a tape of my voice so that the actor speaking my part on taping day would sound somewhat like me. I knew that would be impossible. In South Africa they nicknamed me the South Carolina redneck preacher. That is just what *Unshackled* received!

I finally sent the finished testimony form to them and the voice tapings. Sister Flossie called me on several occasions, making a few adjustments where needed. Several weeks later I received a call from her and she said they were taping my testimony and it was being produced for the Pacific Garden Missions Unshackled Program. Wow! My heart fell to my feet. I began to pray that God would use my testimony to change lives.

It was not long after the live taping that Sister McNeil called me and gave me the airing date. February 7-13, 1999. It was a thirty-minute testimony #2512. She told me to spread the word! I told my pastor, Mike Hamlet, and he shared it with our church family at First Baptist North Spartanburg. My wife Diane said "Testimony number 2512, notice the #12? It is your Spartanburg High School Football number! Now, that is God!"

Months later Sister McNeil called and said a large number of people calling from around the world were touched by my testimony. She asked if it was okay to air it again. I told her to air it as often as they liked. It is to give glory to God, because Jesus is Lord!

Lesson learned: God is the God who opens doors.
Revelation 3:8

JOHNNY HARLOW

How can I begin telling you about a man who had such a powerful influence on my spiritual life and especially my worship? If you were ever in his presence you know what I am talking about. His laughter would fill a room with great expectation and you love to join in laughter with him.

Psalm 96:9 O, worship the Lord in the beauty of holiness: fear before him, all the earth.

I remember going to Atlanta and singing with the First Baptist North Choir during the Southern Baptist Convention. I am not a singer by a long stretch, so he told me to join the choir and just say "watermelon" for every word of the song. I agreed to do this, but I soon realized he wanted every song memorized. Well, there went the watermelon singing.

Yes, it is none other than Johnny Harlow, the dynamic worship leader at First North, taking us to a room to sit and meditate on the music, the Lord and a self inspection of our heart before singing at his great convention. Again, it is hard to explain that moment, but a holy hush came over the orchestra and the choir. The spot light of God was shining on us and we were overtaken by HIS presence. I was trembling and weeping and I heard others doing the same. Johnny believed we didn't need to start until the Spirit was finished with His work, in us. That day something happened to me and I learned something about worship. Pray and purify yourself before singing the Lord's songs. A True God Moment!

We left the prayer room with much humility and headed to our spot on stage to worship the Lord at the convention, in song. I was glad I learned the songs because Johnny called me to sing on the front line and I must admit that I was so scared I did use the word "watermelon" several times.

My heart was crushed when I got the news that Johnny was sick and in the hospital. I remember the choir going and singing to him on the Spartanburg Regional Hospital lawn. I can't sing but I was trying to sing with my whole heart to a man who taught me how to worship. Many members of our church went and prayed for Johnny because we loved him and wanted him well.

One day I went to visit Johnny in the hospital and I asked if I could pray for him. He said yes, and I began to pray for God to heal my precious friend. After praying Johnny looked at me and with tender words said, "Dave, thank you for praying for me, but remember this: Philippians 3:10 says, 'that I may know Him, and the power of His resurrection, and the fellowship of His suffering, being made conformable unto his death'." When I heard him speak these words I knew he would not be with us much longer. I wept.

I pause even now as I write this and thank God for putting Johnny Harlow into my lie. His laughter, the Twin Living Christmas Trees, The Passion, his heart for worship, his love for his church, his choir, and his orchestra, his family and his heart to see souls saved, changed my life.

Psalm 29:2 Give unto the Lord the glory due unto His name; worship the Lord in the beauty of holiness.

I wish you could have known Johnny Harlow. A man full of joy, love, longsuffering, gentleness, firm, committed to family and sold out to Jesus. A man full of passion for people and carried a special anointing to lead his choir in worship. He started with 44 people in the choir his first week at church and spent hours growing and developing his choir into an enrollment of 350, and 50 in the orchestra. He taught hundreds of children and students in the music ministry. God was with Johnny and his passion for worship changed all of our lives. His legacy lives on in the hearts of those he led so faithfully as our Minister of Music at First North from 1986-2002.

Johnny holds a special place in my heart as we poured our hearts out to one another.

Thank you Johnny, for investing in my life.

1998 REVIVALS

1 John 1:3 We are telling you about what we ourselves have actually seen and heard, so that you may have fellowship with us.

April 16, 1989
Locust Fort Baptist in Locust Fort Alabama was praying for a mighty move of God for their area. Pastors Ron and Betty Foshee were agreeing with their congregation.

Revival days are here and God is with those two preaching deacons from South Carolina. The fire of God blazed through this church as 120 souls were saved. The school across the street from the church opened its doors for Don to share his prison testimony. We later learned that Joe Hazelrig, Superintendent of the school system, had given the okay for Don to speak.

The students listened to this incredible testimony; "From Pharmacy to Prison, to Preacher." There was not a dry eye among the students. They were invited to the closing night of the revival at the church. That night the church was packed wall to wall and was beyond overflowing. Teenagers brought out chairs, the choir was packed, chairs filled the aisle, but most of all, God showed up and more souls entered into the Kingdom of God that night.

April 12, 1998
Several years later Pastor Ron Foshee was pasturing Ryans Creek Baptist in Bremen, Alabama. He invited us to conduct a revival at this church. Philip Porter would fly to this meeting in his twin engine Barron plane. They would land at Folsom Airport and Larry and Jerry Wilson from the church would pick us up at 7pm on Saturday night.

Excitement and anticipation filled the atmosphere. During Sunday school 20 were saved. The preaching was blazing hot and the altars were filled each night of the revival. The door to the high school opened as principle Mickey opened the door for us to speak to the entire school assembly. The students received the message well, and night after night young people filled the church.

On youth night, 66 young people prayed to receive Jesus! Wednesday night ten more souls were saved. One young man named Zackery was delivered from Witchcraft and was influential in winning six of his friends to Jesus.

When the dust of revival settled 89 people had received Jesus. It was a time of harvest and truly God's timing for His people. You can't explain it. It is just God meeting with His people as they cried out in prayers before revival, and they watched Him answer their prayers.

May 12, 1998 ... Romania

A large group of us from First North Church headed to Romania and we were excited about having the opportunity to speak in churches and to serve in some street ministry in the country of Romania. We hoped to meet with missionaries Mike and Kathy Kemper, Adi, Daniel, and Rev. Tolas.

Our plane arrived in Burcharest just as the sun was rising over the city, and the farm land was beautiful. It was May 13th now, and I was ready to visit with the people of Romania.

My room, number 412, was at Hotel Central and my roommate was Allen Thompson. Our bellhop was Adrian. He speaks English well enough. I learned Adrian is 20 years old and he works two jobs. His is very polite and is always eager to help us with our bags.

As I often do, I start small conversations in hopes of getting an inroad to share my testimony. The door did open and I told him my life story. I asked Adrian if he would like to pray to invite Jesus into his heart and become a Christian. He immediately prayed! Jesus forgave him of his sins.

Adrian was my first convert on Romanian soil. I removed my witnessing bracelet and gave it to him so he could share his new faith. The next day he told he had prayed with three of his friends to receive Jesus. I knew I was in the middle of God's will being in Romania.

TWO MEN OF FAITH

REV. TERRY WHITESIDES AND REV. DON MOORE

It is amazing how God puts people into your life to fulfill His mission. Rev. Don Moore, now in Heaven, and Rev. Terry Whitesides are men I have partnered in ministry to feed the hungry, just like Jesus asked us to do. After feeding the poor in Nicaragua for years, I have joined forces with these two men of God to help feed the poor in Brevard, North Carolina, and Jonesville, South Carolina. I have never met men more dedicated to feeding the poor and helping the hurting come to know Jesus. Their tireless efforts with getting the food, and then the distribution of the food, are amazing.

They have about 60 volunteers who have the same work ethic and compassion to work long hours to help the hurting in their cities. Each invited me to preach and teach God's Word to the clients on each day of distribution. The Lord is touching many lives for His kingdom. Currently we are seeing as many as 3,500 clients per month and the Lord Jesus continues to meet all of their needs.

Special thanks to Sister Della Hill and her force of volunteers who work in Jonesville, South Carolina. Della says, "It is done from a heart of love!"

We are most grateful. Rev. Terry Whitesides is a soul winner. Many souls are being saved at his church (Crossroads Baptist), because he is feeding the poor and showing God's love. He is a man on fire for Jesus and I have been in prayer with him and have seen his tears and his broken heart over lost souls.

Rev. Don Moore taught me much about "faith." Sometimes enough food is difficult to get, especially when you are serving so many people. Often I would watch Brother Don crying out to God for help, and the phone would ring, and the person on the phone would say, "I have 100 turkeys I am bringing by the food ministry."

Rev. Don was also a great soul winner and I learned a lot by watching these two giants of faith love on the hurting.

I want to thank them from the bottom of my heart for showing me Jesus in their everyday lives.

Rev. Terry Whitesides, Dave Walton, and Don Moore
Hollyanne

CONGRATULATIONS

Alexander "BUCK" Walton

(fight name) ***BUCK Earnhart***

LOVE,
David Odell Walton
Gloria Sue Walton Wood
Boyd Lee Walton
James Stanley Walton
Evelyn Kay Walton Walden

THANKS DAD FOR ALL THE MEMORIES!

{ Matthew 6:9-13 }

Congratulations, Dad for your 2012 Induction into the Carolinas Boxing Hall of Fame.

"For God so loved the world, that he gave his only begotten Son, that whosoever believeth in Him should not perish but have everlasting life."

—John 3:16

Alexander "Buck" Walton

Congratulations on your 2012 induction into the Carolinas Boxing Hall of Fame

— Thank you —

For all you have done for your community in coaching young people in football, baseball and boxing. Your championship teams continue to be talked about, even today.

Stan Walton, Danny Pearson, Steve Pearson, Monte Moore, Wayne Casasanta, Don Stanley, Bob Tallant, Shorty, The Beacon Drive-In, Spartan Mill Hill Boys...

DADDY'S GRADUATION DAY
Journal by Dave's Sister, Kay

DADDY'S PROMOTION TO HEAVEN – THE FINAL DAY – SEPTEMBER 29, 1994
OUR SISTER SUE – WAITING AND WATCHING

As I mentioned at the beginning, Thursday, September 29, 1994 was a beautiful, sunny day. Earlier that morning my three brothers, Dave, Boyd, and Stan; and my sister Sue and I would wake up and decide we would not be going to work that day. And yet neither of us knew the others had made this decision. God was directing our steps for sure! One by one we all five made it to Mama and Daddy's.

The Hospice nurse came that morning, checked Daddy, and left. A childhood friend (Don Stanley) and ministry partner for many years of Dave's came by for a short visit with Daddy and the family, and left. We had been told by the nurse different phases we would see taking place during this journey. This was so very helpful and kept us aware of the time. It is like God spoke to each of us that morning and we all knew Daddy would be going home to be with Jesus and we were not going to miss being there with him and our mother.

As the morning slowly ticked by, we noticed our sister Sue had made her way to the living room and was camped out by Daddy's bedside. We also noticed that no one else seemed to be dropping by. All five of us grown kids were there with Mama and Daddy. The nurse had told us it could be a few hours to a day. We had also been made aware weeks earlier when someone is sleeping most of the time it could be at the end they will open their eyes, and have a minute or so before they depart. From the moment we heard this we believed and hoped we would see Daddy do just that.

The rest of us have decided we're going to have a bite of lunch. So we're in kitchen deciding on a sandwich, or a sweet, and getting something to drink. And Sue is staying close by Daddy's side. It was not yet noon. A different one would go in and check momentarily. I had decided on a dessert and had sat down at the end of the table when all of a sudden we heard our sister say, ***"His eyes are open!"***
We all rushed through the door to the living room like a herd of cattle to see Daddy!

IT WAS AMAZING! There we were. All seven of us together for this moment in time and Daddy's eyes are open! I remember Stan is on my side of the bed, Dave is at the foot of the bed, and I believe Mama, Sue, and Boyd are on the other side. Daddy is scanning from left to right taking in glimpses of us, and we are speaking words of love to him, one at a time, and all at the same time. I remember Stan telling Daddy he loved him and telling him God had sent him a 747 jet to take him home. I was hearing I love you, and See you in heaven! And we were gazing into Daddy's eyes and it was amazing!

And then, it happened, our precious Daddy took his last breath. It was 12:07p.m.
Daddy had a smile on his face. I knew he was at peace and with Jesus. He was now well and whole.
How could I ask for more than that?

Psalm 116:15 "Precious in the sight of the Lord is the death of his saints..."

Love & blessings,
Your sis, KAY

September 29, 1994. The time was 12:06 pm. Daddy moved to Heaven.

A WORD FROM DIANE WALTON

I have been married to Dave Walton for forty-eight years. We met at the Beacon Restaurant in June of 1966. We married in May of 1969. I have watched him grow in the Lord over the years. I see all the things that make him a wonderful husband, father, Poppi, and evangelist. His kindness, gentleness, compassion, and love for hurting people are very real. He is always talking about winning souls in the streets and I have been with him on several soul-winning ventures in restaurants. As a matter of fact, he has trained me and I have also had the privilege of leading several waitresses to Jesus. We have traveled into Nicaragua together on 17 mission trips. He is exciting to be with and I go as often as possible to his revivals.

Dave has conducted over 700 meetings and I have traveled with him on many revival meetings. Each time, seeing God use Dave in incredible ways. He is a man on fire for Jesus and I am a witness to this 24/7 because he dreams it, studies it, and goes out weekly searching for lost souls.

What touches my heart the most about Dave is that I know he is a broken man. Together we have been through difficult days and he always encourages me to trust God. I have witnessed his tears flowing down his face over lost friends and family members. When he prays, I know God is listening.

When I see him preaching and praying, I see a man who has much depth in the Lord. He has faced mountains, heart attacks, depression, and defeats in his life, but his face reflects a bittersweet past. He has shared many of his failures with me, but he continues to hold on to his faith and hope for the future.

I pray for Dave daily because he does not know how to slow down. He seems to have one speed, RACE, full steam ahead. I write these things about him and I brag on him a lot, but he always gives the credit to Jesus. That is why I love him so much!

Just a few closing thoughts: He is a hard worker, trying to always make things better for his family, church, friends and our beloved country. Dave is a giver and never expects anything in return. He is committed to Bible study, devotions, prayer, winning souls, loving God and journaling the events that God does through him.

He is a fascinating guy to be married to for 48 years. I praise God that we can share our lives through ministry. Seeking to fulfill God's plan and purpose in our lives, I ask you please pray for Dave Walton and our family, as we press on to brag on Jesus, and win souls until our last breath. Our greatest desire is to win the Soul Winner's Crown and lay it at the feet of Jesus.

Diane Walton

Dave Walton Ministries wants to hear from you.
Tell us your amazing testimony.
Take a moment to brag on Jesus.
Our mailing address is:

Dave Walton Ministries
P.O. Box 349
Roebuck, SC 29376

A VERY SPECIAL PLACE HENAGAR, ALABAMA

Sand Mountain, they call it, is one of my favorite places on earth. Friends like Winston and Faye Nell Wilks, Alan and Kathy Wilks, Kevin and Karen Wilks, Wint and Kristy Wilks, and David and Dale Starling played an important part in the ministry of Dave Walton Evangelistic Association. I am forever thankful.

Nearly every time we are in Henagar, Alabama we stay in the home of Winston and Faye Nell Wilks. They treat Diane and I like family.

Mr. Winston is a dedicated man-of-God and a tremendous family man.

Faye Nell Wilks is an incredible woman-of-God and is deeply involved at her home church, Henagar Baptist. By the way, she is an amazing cook! I love her fried okra, cakes, cornbread...you get the picture.

This group of friends has prayed Diane and I through some tough times. My heart overflows with gratefulness to God for allowing our lives to intercept, many years ago.

I want to personally thank each one of these followers of Jesus for standing with me in ministry, support, and prayers.

We send each of you our deepest love wrapped with prayers!

Diane and Dave Walton

GO!

Made in the
USA
Columbia, SC